Modern Japan: A Very Short Introduction

VERY SHORT INTRODUCTIONS are for anyone wanting a stimulating and accessible way into a new subject. They are written by experts, and have been translated into more than 45 different languages.

The series began in 1995, and now covers a wide variety of topics in every discipline. The VSI library now contains over 500 volumes—a Very Short Introduction to everything from Psychology and Philosophy of Science to American History and Relativity—and continues to grow in every subject area.

Titles in the series include the following:

Christopher Goto-Jones

MODERN JAPAN

A Very Short Introduction

OXFORD

UNIVERSITY PRESS

Great Clarendon Street, Oxford OX2 6DP

Oxford University Press is a department of the University of Oxford.
It furthers the University's objective of excellence in research, scholarship,
and education by publishing worldwide in

Oxford New York

Auckland Cape Town Dar es Salaam Hong Kong Karachi
Kuala Lumpur Madrid Melbourne Mexico City Nairobi
New Delhi Shanghai Taipei Toronto

With offices in

Argentina Austria Brazil Chile Czech Republic France Greece
Guatemala Hungary Italy Japan Poland Portugal Singapore
South Korea Switzerland Thailand Turkey Ukraine Vietnam

Oxford is a registered trade mark of Oxford University Press
in the UK and in certain other countries

Published in the United States
by Oxford University Press Inc., New York

© Christopher Goto-Jones 2009

The moral rights of the author have been asserted
Database right Oxford University Press (maker)

First published 2009

All rights reserved. No part of this publication may be reproduced,
stored in a retrieval system, or transmitted, in any form or by any means,
without the prior permission in writing of Oxford University Press,
or as expressly permitted by law, or under terms agreed with the appropriate
reprographics rights organization. Enquiries concerning reproduction
outside the scope of the above should be sent to the Rights Department,
Oxford University Press, at the address above

You must not circulate this book in any other binding or cover
and you must impose the same condition on any acquirer

British Library Cataloguing in Publication Data

Data available

Library of Congress Cataloging in Publication Data

Data available

Typeset by SPI Publisher Services, Pondicherry, India

Printed and bound by
CPI Group (UK) Ltd, Croydon, CR0 4YY

ISBN 978-0-19-923569-8

Contents

Acknowledgements and conventions

Japanese names are written in their proper order, with family name preceding given name. In the case of a number of important historical figures, it is conventional to refer to them by their given names: hence, Tokugawa Ieyasu is often known simply as Ieyasu; Oda Nobunaga is known as Nobunaga; Toyotomi Hideyoshi is known as Hideyoshi. However, these are exceptions to the norm. Long vowels have been indicated by a macron, as in 'Nishida Kitarô', although macrons have not been used for words commonly seen in English, as in 'Tokyo'. Japanese does not mark plurals with an s, hence *samurai*, *daimyo* etc. are both singular and plural.

I would like to thank Rana Mitter, Rikki Kersten, Angus Lockyer, and the anonymous reviewers at Oxford University Press for reading the complete manuscript, for their generous and constructive criticisms, and for their understanding about the difficulties of writing such a Very Small Book. Nonetheless, responsibility for all the confusions and any errors is entirely my own. I also owe a debt of gratitude to my editor at the Press, Andrea Keegan, whose persistent encouragement and patience with me (especially after a complete hard-disk failure in Osaka) were remarkable. Thanks, too, to the Modern East Asia Research Centre (MEARC) for funding a period in Kyoto to actually do the writing, and to Esther for conjuring the time out of nowhere.

And finally, thanks to Nozomi and the rest of the farm, as well as to my students in Leiden, who have instilled in me the importance of explaining rather than assuming; I hope that this little book is a step in the right direction, although I daren't assume so.

Really, this book is for my parents, who have always supported my interest in Japan without really knowing why it was interesting: I hope this helps.

List of illustrations

Introduction: what's modern about modern Japan?

For many people today, modern Japan is best recognized as an economic powerhouse. According to many commentators, Japan is today's most successful industrial (or even post-industrial) economy, combining almost unprecedented affluence with remarkable social stability and apparent harmony. Despite its recent economic troubles, and despite the rapid rise of China, Japan remains the second largest economy on the planet according to most indicators, behind only the United States. Japanese goods and cultural products are consumed all over the world, ranging from animated movies and Playstation games, to cars and semiconductors, to management techniques and the martial arts.

In many ways, this image of Japan makes it into an icon of 'modernity' in the contemporary world, and yet the nation itself remains something of an enigma to many non-specialists, who see it as a confusing montage of the alien and the familiar, the traditional and the modern, and even the 'Eastern' and the 'Western'. As we will see, part of the reason for this confusion lies in the assumption that whilst modernity generates little cultural dissonance in the so-called 'West', in Japan and elsewhere the trappings of modernity appear incongruous or even inexplicable. At the base of this assumption is the deeply felt entanglement of modernity with European and American history. Indeed, this perceived entanglement is at the core of many of the world's contemporary protests against globalization and capitalism: to many people the steamroller of the modern looks like the expansion of the West.

As an example, let's pause to consider a recent spectacle.

Perceptions of modern Japan: FIFA World Cup 2002

There was a measure of European scepticism when Japan and Korea were chosen to co-host the 2002 FIFA World Cup finals. Was the first World Cup in Asia going to be another World Cup like USA 1994, when it was hosted by a rich country that didn't really know anything about football (or 'soccer') in an attempt to make it more popular there? The European public knew even less about these 'Far Eastern' nations than they knew about the USA: they knew about Nintendo, Sony, and Daewoo; they knew about karate and taekwondo; they knew about Pearl Harbor, Hiroshima, and the Korean War. They didn't know that Japan's 'J-League' was one of the world's most lucrative football leagues; and they certainly didn't know that Korea would make it through to the semi-finals (where they would lose to Germany), having beaten the 'Great Powers' of Italy and Spain on their way, finishing above pre-tournament favourites such as England, Argentina, and the reigning champions, France. In general, the tremendous passion for (and ability in) football in Japan and Korea took Europe by surprise.

It is interesting to reflect on why the scale of interest in football in East Asia was surprising to so many people. A partial answer resides in the kinds of popular images of Japan to which the 'Western' public have been exposed. During its coverage of the World Cup, for example, the venerable BBC produced two beautiful advertising sequences for the games. The first, screened in the weeks preceding the games, was a two-minute segment in the style of 'anime', the virally popular medium of Japanese animation that currently accounts for 60% of all televised cartoons in the world. The short film commenced with a dramatic voice-over that would be familiar to fans of 'beat 'em up' video games and martial arts movies: 'Every four years great heroes come from the four corners of the earth to compete for the greatest prize known to man . . . '. In the background, a stylized flicker of kanji (Chinese characters used in Japan) and hangul (Korean characters) pulsed ominously. Then the advert exploded into life as a science-fictional spectacle: a ball is kicked into the air like a rocket; computer screens and neon lights flash and beep as they trace it; a futuristic flotation tank holds a man with a gleaming, metallic cyborg leg (he turns out to be the superhumanly talented French captain, Zidane); and then a flurry of anime football heroes (none of whom are Japanese or Korean) flash through the streets of a neon-riddled (Japanese) city in pursuit of the rocket.

The two-minute commercial was slick and stylized, full of references to popular culture, and riddled with implications that Japan was somehow a cool and futuristic utopia, a science-fictional realm of cyborgs and computerization of the kind that William Gibson famously depicted in his cyberpunk classic, *Neuromancer* (1984). In addition, none of the actual football seemed to involve anyone from Japan or Korea, although there were lots of people in the streets watching the foreign football-heroes appreciatively.

The second sequence was screened during the opening credits of every match. This was a much more romantic montage of images: beginning slowly with a temple on a lake at sunrise, followed by a close-up of the eyes of a Buddha statue, a fluttering Japanese flag, some sumo wrestlers, a fluttering Korean flag, and then some koi carp. At this point, a football is kicked into a light-blur that then guides us through the rest of the images: Buddha again, a cityscape (with neon lights and a temple), a football stadium (with a Brazilian player), some traditional Korean dancing, David Beckham, some more Korean dancing, another sumo wrestler, another temple, a lingering shot of a *geisha* (or *gisaeng*), and then a slow romantic shot of Mount Fuji. At this point there is a sudden change of pace, as though we are being brought into the modern era: a Shinkansen bullet-train explodes into view, more unidentified footballers, more trains, more neon lights and crowded streets with illuminated screens (showing footballers), more traditional Korean dancing, and finally the ball-blur flashes between the uprights of a great *torii* (sacred Shintô gateway) as though it were a goal.

Of course, the imagery here is clichéd and unimaginative, but this is precisely why it reveals so much about the ways in which Japan is represented in the so-called West. Leaving aside the bizarre absence of Japanese football players in these commercials, we see a characteristic mixture of traditional culture (sumo, *geisha*, Fuji, Buddhist icons) and hyper-modernity (bullet-trains, neon cities, cyborgs), of the mysterious and the technological. Japan is represented as an enigmatically different 'other' that has somehow appropriated (and then transformed) the trappings of modernity that should be so familiar to a Western audience. The audience is supposed to be affected by seeing a sumo wrestler and a high-speed train in the same sequence. But why should this have an impact?

The point here is that it is not only Japan's cultural difference that makes it so intriguing, but also the fact that it is simultaneously a modern, technologically advanced, non-Western nation. At this vulgar level of analysis, Japan is presented as intriguing because it has a rich history of 'Eastern' traditions and an oddly 'Western' present: modernity and the West being difficult for the audience (or for the BBC) to disentangle.

In other words, the questions of the meaning and integrity of modernity gives the interested observer an extra reason to consider Japan, which is widely regarded as being the first modern 'non-Western' nation in history. Indeed, the history of modern Japan, since the end of its apparent international isolation in the mid-19th century to the present day, is the document of a nation grappling with the effects of its encounter with Western powers and its simultaneous exposure to the ideas and technologies of modernity. Negotiation, both in the political and intellectual senses, has been a key feature of this period. Indeed, the experience of Japan provides us with a fascinating lens on the myriad ways in which nations respond to the complex problems of cultural, intellectual, social, political, and scientific change, especially as occasioned by the sudden (and uninvited) arrival of American gunboats.

This *Very Short Introduction* to *Modern Japan* cannot hope to serve as an adequate general survey of this exciting and important period in Japan's history. Instead, it will consider a series of questions about what it means to call Japan a 'modern' society and what this category of 'modern' has meant to different groups of Japanese people at different times. Along the way, it will challenge a number of common assumptions about Japanese history, such as the frequent claim that Japan was completely isolated from the outside world during its long period of isolation, or *sakoku* (17th to 19th centuries), and hence that openness to other cultures was itself a key feature of Japanese modernity. We will consider some of the ways in which cultural and social continuity and change interact through the period, even over apparent singularities such as the catastrophic conclusion to World War II in the Pacific, hence challenging the assumption that postwar Japan is somehow discontinuous with its own traditions.

And finally, although much of the material here will inevitably focus on the ways in which political, intellectual, and social elites engaged with the profound transformations of Japanese society and the question of its modernity, there is also a need to look at the ways in which these changes were experienced by the people at large, not merely as the passive recipients of grand historical trends but also as active agents involved in shaping their modern nation for themselves. In some ways this tendency towards national self-determination is one of the key features (and core problematics) of modernity.

In other words, this is a little book about the ways in which Japan has engaged with modernity, but it is also a book about the ways in which the experience of Japan should help us to reconsider the meaning and dimensions of the 'modern' itself. It is not the case that modernity *happened to* Japan, but rather through industry, toil, bloodshed, and creativity Japan forged itself into the thriving, modern nation that we know today. Whilst the meaning of the modern remains controversial and contested, the example of Japan helps to illustrate the necessity of encompassing the varied experiences of many different nations when trying to understand its dimensions and historical

1. A rooftop Shintô shrine

reality. Modernity and the West may be related, but they are not identical.

What is 'modern' anyway?

It is a common (mis)conception that 'modern' is essentially a temporal or historical term, referring to a period of time that is close to the present. Whilst this meaning may serve in everyday usage, it is much more interesting and useful to consider a more technical and substantive sense of the term. In this framework, the term 'modern' refers to a more-or-less specific constellation of intellectual, social, political, and scientific norms and practices. By identifying the modern as a cluster of related principles rather than as merely a period, we are able to trace its occurrence in different periods in different national or cultural settings: was Europe modern before Japan, for instance? Was Japan modern before Russia? If so, why? It also enables us to ask provocative questions about the present: is Japan modern and, if so, how can we explain why it looks so different from, say, the United Kingdom? To paraphrase this important question: which elements of the modern are essential, and which are culturally contingent? And finally, if the occurrence of the modern can be observed in this way, does it become possible to identify conditions that are somehow 'postmodern'? Is the modern already in the past in some places, and not in the present at all? Are there locations where it remains in the future?

This approach opens up some rather dangerous ethical problems: if we accept that the modern is effectively a stage of development, how can we avoid (and should we avoid) *judging* the development of nations against these standards? In other words, does the idea of the modern smuggle in a linear conception of historical progress that culminates in contemporary Euro-American ideals? As we will see in Chapter 3, these questions were of vital concern to Japanese intellectuals as early as the 1940s, as they struggled to find ways to 'overcome modernity'. This call to overcome the modern was related in complicated ways to Japan's project of empire-building in Asia. In the postwar period, it becomes linked to calls for Japan and Asia to 'say no' to the USA.

Given how important the concept of the 'modern' appears to be, what can be said about its meaning and content? Unfortunately, there remains a lack of consensus about the exact dimensions of the modern, although most commentators agree about the kinds of symptoms that we should be able to use to diagnose it. A society might be considered modern, for instance, if it exhibits signs of industrialization and urbanization. An economic system might be modern if it boasts a market economy organized according to capitalist principles. A modern political system should be organized around a central nation-state, supported by popular nationalism, and a representative system of government (perhaps a democracy) that gives voice to the will of the people. This political system rests upon a so-called 'modern consciousness' that involves an awareness of the dignity of individuals and their inalienable rights. It supposes a level of literacy and access to information (via education and the public sphere) that enables people to make rational choices about their best interests. This emphasis on rationality is foundational: the modern era is held to be characterized by reason rather than superstition (or perhaps religion) and by the development of science and technology – the mechanization of society. Modern man holds the technological power to attempt to control nature, to unleash destructive weapons, and to save lives through modern medicine. Industrial machines make the world smaller and provide the conditions of the possibility of a meaningfully global world: the train is the pervasive harbinger of modern times.

Many of these characteristics seem to find their origins in the European Enlightenment of the 18th century, and this is no coincidence since this is where many commentators locate the genesis of the modern. In particular, the concept of the modern seems to share the Enlightenment project's faith in progress and its aspirations towards the universalism of its maxims. However, it is important to remember that there is a difference between observing the historical origins of this cluster of ideas in Europe and claiming that the ideas themselves are somehow *essentially* European possessions. Indeed, to make such a claim would run rather counter to the universal spirit of the Enlightenment. Nonetheless, both advocates and opponents of the global spread of modernity, within Europe and outside, have often affected this confusion. It might be better to see the modern condition in the various possible responses to a *world* of capitalist industry.

As we will see, the history of modern Japan contains a variety of positions on this important political question, ranging from those who sought to reject all the trappings of modernity in the name of rejecting Westernization, via those who sought to retain Japanese traditions whilst adopting the 'value-free' aspects of modern rationality, to those who advocated abandoning Japanese traditions entirely on the basis that only by becoming Western could Japan become truly modern. In some ways, this kind of sociocultural anxiety about identity and the place of tradition in society is one of the marks of the modern era, not only in Japan but everywhere. The modern era is not only characterized by great advances in science, but also by social anomie and political unrest.

Indeed, for many, it is precisely this dynamic interplay between the traditional and the modern that makes the process of modernization so exciting and vexatious. In some respects, the modern is conceptualized as the opposite of tradition – the overcoming of traditional (that is, 'irrational') ways of organizing life. However, it would be an extreme interpretation to argue that the modern era should dispense with cultural traditions altogether – George Orwell has famously painted a picture of the probable result of such thinking, in his novel *Nineteen Eighty-Four*. In other words, the modern era should not see an end to cultural diversity, but modern people should engage with their traditions in a transformed way: they should be recognized *as traditions*, rather than *as truths*.

Nonetheless, the process of negotiating a stable and healthy relationship between the traditional and the modern is fraught with difficulties, not least because there is no culture-free standard of modernity against which to measure success. Like it or not, most commentators tend to fall back on the legacy of the European Enlightenment as the prototype, and at that moment we run back into the danger of imperialism. Hence, a key issue for modern times is to learn how to identify the modern when we see it, even if it looks different from our experience, otherwise we risk judging all cultural difference as being evidence of stunted modernity.

Structure of this book

This book is organized more-or-less chronologically. Chapter 1 tackles Japan's simultaneous encounter with the Western world, as US Commodore Perry arrives in 1853 to open the 'isolationist' Japan to international trade, and with currents of modern ideas and social forces that were already developing within Japan during the Tokugawa period: the modern and the Western overlap here, but they are not identical. Japan's emergent modernity is its own. This chapter deals with an often overlooked but vital part of the story of modern Japan: continuities with the past.

Chapter 2 moves into the Meiji period, showing how Japan endeavoured to transform itself into a modern, imperial nation in the second half of the 19th century. This period, sometimes referred to as the Japanese Enlightenment, sees the Japanese enthusiastically embrace modernity and its trappings. Chapter 3 moves forward into the early 20th century and Japan's emergence as a great imperial power in Asia, defeating China (1895) and Russia (1905), and then building a vast empire in the so-called Great East Asia War. The chapter focuses particularly on the ways in which this imperial project was fuelled by (and opposed by) the development of modern industries and political ideas. One key feature of this period was the way in which certain influential intellectuals and political leaders sought to define Japan's wars as attempts to overcome the modern.

Chapter 4 is concerned with the end of World War II, the Allied Occupation, and Japan's rapid economic growth in the postwar period. It discusses the various social and political reforms that were made at that time, with a particular focus on the ways in which Japanese society and culture sought to make sense of the new postwar reality, perhaps moving towards a postmodern identity.

Chapter 5 is a discussion of Japan's identity and role in the post-Cold War world, with a focus on the critical question of Japan's capacity and will to resolve the issues of its imperial legacy and its 'victim consciousness'. These remain 'living issues' in contemporary Japan and determine its quest for 'normalcy' in the international system.

Finally, an epilogue looks at what it means to live in Japan at the start of the 21st century.

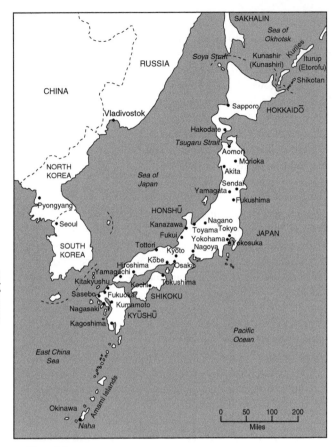

2. Map of Japan

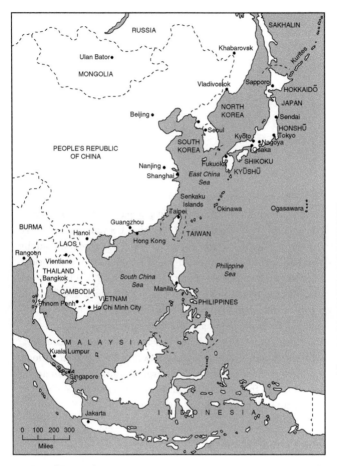

3. Map of East Asia

Chapter 1

Japan's encounter with the modern world

At first glance, the origins of modern Japan seem to coincide conveniently with the dramatic arrival of US Commodore Perry in 1853. Before his arrival, Japan looked like a feudal monarchy that had been hiding in self-imposed isolation from the world for 250 years; within 50 years of his visit Japan had literally undergone a revolution – it had a modern, industrial economy, a constitutional government, and the beginnings of a colonial empire. To many commentators, this astonishingly rapid transformation was occasioned by Japan's shocking encounter with the superior technology and power of the Western nations. In this version of the story, Perry broke traditional Japan and forced it into the modern world. However, as we will see in this chapter, the reality is not so simple.

The arrival of Perry

After the annexation of Texas in 1845, the war with Mexico, and finally the incorporation of California into the Union in September 1850 during the so-called 'gold rush', the USA was expanding westwards energetically. The imperial ambitions of the USA and its desire to compete with Great Britain for lucrative trade opportunities in Asia encouraged it to look even further west across the Pacific Ocean to Japan. In this spirit, the arrival of Commodore Matthew Perry with his four fabled 'black ships' in July 1853 seemed like a natural step in the process.

Perry was famous in naval circles for his passion for modernization, and particularly steam-powered ships; even before he had made his first, famous trip to Japan in the *USS Mississippi* he had already earned the epithet 'the father of the steam-navy'. It is not without significance, therefore, that it was the presence of four black steam-ships that intimidated the local government officials in Uraga Bay (near Edo, present-day Tokyo) to take the unprecedented step of allowing Perry to come ashore and present a letter from US President Millard Fillmore. Until that time, an official policy of isolationism (*sakoku*) meant that foreigners had been forbidden from the mainland of Japan, with only a small number of Dutch traders permitted to stay on the tiny, artificial islet of Deshima near the outlying city of Nagasaki since 1641. The letter contained a series of demands for more open trade with Japan, and Perry left Uraga with the ominous promise to return the next year with a more substantial naval force, ready to force compliance if it was not forthcoming.

In fact, the USA was a later comer: European ships had been trying to crack open Japan for at least the previous 50 years. Russian vessels started to show interest in the northerly island of Hokkaido as early as 1792. Already developing a serious stake in China, the British sailed to Uraga Bay in 1818 to make a half-hearted request for the opening of trade relations, but their advances were rejected. In 1825, the shogunate government, or *bakufu*, became so concerned about the appearance of foreign vessels that it issued the order that coastal warlords should expel foreign advances by force if necessary, and in 1837 a US merchant ship was shelled. Indeed, for the first 50 years of the 19th century, the *bakufu* really believed that it could keep the Western world out. It was not until an emissary of the Dutch King William III in 1844 tried to explain to the shogun that the world had changed since the expulsion of the Europeans in the 17th century that the *bakufu* really started to rethink its place in the world. Comprehensive British victories over China in the so-called Opium Wars in 1842 seemed to prove the point. If the British could humiliate the colossus of China so effectively, how could the smaller and more peripheral nation of Japan escape a similar fate? Lest they provoke serious military retaliation from the Western powers, the *bakufu* quickly rescinded its order to fire on foreign vessels. It was in this context that Perry first arrived in Uraga Bay.

When Perry returned with nine ships in February 1854, he found government officials willing to sign the Treaty of Kanagawa (31 March 1854). This treaty opened the ports of Shimoda and Hakodate, and also provided for the stationing of the first US consul on mainland Japan; Townsend Harris would take up this post in Shimoda in July 1856. The Treaty of Kanagawa opened the floodgates, and the European imperial powers quickly secured similar deals: France, Britain, the Netherlands, and Russia all signed new treaties in the wake of Perry's return.

By 1858, the so-called Unequal Treaties regime was firmly in place: without a shot being fired, Japan found itself in a similar position to China after the Opium Wars (with the notable exception that the Western powers agreed to prohibit opium trade with Japan). Japan had lost control of its tariffs, had opened its borders to trade and commerce with the West, and had even granted the privilege of extra-territoriality to the Western powers (which meant that foreign nationals were exempt from Japanese law even on Japanese soil). Rather than being justified by military defeat, however, these measures were imposed on Japan on the basis that it was not an equal member of international society – it was not a modern, industrial, constitutional polity. As we will see, this humiliation was itself a powerful force fuelling the development of a strong sense of nationalism in late 19th-century Japan, as well as a key factor driving the revolution to come. At all costs, Japan sought to end the Unequal Treaties.

It is important to note that it would be an exaggeration to argue that these humiliations damaged a coherent or pre-existing sense of national pride in Japan, since prior to the mid-19th century Japan was a relatively divided, fragmented, and non-centralized territory, knitted together by bonds of loyalty, military dependency, and religious imagery. Indeed, in many ways, the humiliation of the Unequal Treaties was fundamental in the process of creating a modern sense of national consciousness in Japan.

The significance of the modern, industrial power of Perry's fleet in these events should not be underestimated. Indeed, the image of the 'black ships' quickly became iconic in Japan, representing the menace of Western power as well as the threat of traditional Japan being overcome by the cultural and technological force of modernity. An intriguing anecdote concerning Perry's return to Japan in 1854 illustrates this point: contemporary accounts describe the way in which the Japanese officials arranged for a sumo contest to be staged for the American officers, presumably in an attempt to intimidate the foreigners with the power and martial spirit of the Japanese. However, the US delegation is reported to have been singularly unimpressed by the spectacle, finding the performance laughable. For their part, the US delegation assembled a 100-metre circle of track and made a gift of a quarter-scale steam locomotive for the Japanese officials to ride. It is a testament to the astonishing impact of industrial technology that this toy train was far more intimidating than the primal power of sumo wrestling.

Perry had probably been aware of the effect that his black ships and his little locomotive would have. Before embarking on his mission, Perry had read much of the available literature about Tokugawa Japan, and he is even thought to have

4. Commodore Perry's paddle-steamer arriving in Uraga Bay in 1853, shown in woodblock print

consulted with the famous Japanologist, Philipp Franz von Siebold, who had lived in the Dutch enclave on Deshima for eight years before returning to Leiden in the Netherlands. Nonetheless, information on the secretive and isolationist nation was scarce. Only a tiny number of Westerners had any first-hand knowledge of Japan, and even those who did (like Siebold himself) had only limited exposure to the real social and political circumstances of the unfamiliar land. Orientalism was rife; the romance of the 'mystical East' coloured most accounts. Western accounts of Japan in the early 19th century portrayed it as a feudal kingdom, untouched by the hands of industry and modernity. Most accounts also mentioned how favourably Japan compared to the other 'barbarian peoples' encountered by the European imperialists in Asia and Africa: the Japanese were apparently cultured, clean, and unfailingly polite. Townsend Harris, for instance, famously described Japan as the embodiment of a golden age of simplicity and honesty.

Perry's information was flawed in a number of very important ways. Consider the fact that while Perry knew that Japan was an imperial polity, presided over by an emperor (usually known as the 'Mikado' in the West at the time), he was not aware of the difference between the emperor's court and the shogun's *bakufu* government. Indeed, Perry left Japan in 1854 believing that he had signed a treaty with agents of the emperor, when in fact he had been received by the *bakufu*. This difference was significant and had serious repercussions for the course of modern Japanese history; the institution of the *bakufu* was one of the key characteristics of the Tokugawa political order, setting it apart from the types of feudal monarchy that characterized European history. Even in the late 1850s, US Consul General Townsend Harris persisted in addressing the shogun as 'His Majesty the Emperor of Japan'.

If Perry was confused about something as fundamental as the identity of the sovereign of Japan, about what else might he have been under-informed? In other words, what were the actual characteristics of the Japan that Perry encountered in the 1850s, and was it really as pre-modern as he thought?

The unification of Japan and the making of Pax Tokugawa

Most of the institutions that characterized Japan in the mid-19th century were established at the start of the 17th century by the founders of the Tokugawa regime, after whom the period was named: Tokgugawa Ieyasu, who finally unified Japan following the epic battle of Sekigahara in 1600; and Ieyasu's grandson, Tokugawa Iemitsu, who ruled as shogun from 1623 to 1651.

The Pax Tokugawa followed a long period of internecine warfare called the *sengoku-jidai* (period of the country at war), which began with the Ōnin War (1467–77), when the ancient capital of Kyoto was sacked, and continued until the unification and pacification of Japan by the 'three unifiers', Oda Nobunaga, Toyotomi Hideyoshi, and then Tokugawa Ieyasu, who set up his seat of government in Edo (present-day Tokyo) in the early years of the 17th century. During these centuries of near-constant warfare, Japan witnessed the rise to dominance of the samurai warrior class and their daimyo lords, as well as the agitation of warrior-monks from various Buddhist temples.

The bloody process of unification began with Oda Nobunaga's ruthless expansion from his home province of Owari (near present-day Nagoya). Nobunaga is usually portrayed by historians as brutal and self-interested, and it is certainly true that he violently suppressed the neighbouring villages and destroyed innumerable Buddhist temples, burning their ancient libraries and murdering the monks and their supporters.

However, it would be wrong to present Nobunaga entirely as a brutish tyrant. He established a pattern of loose, feudal rule over semi-autonomous regions combined with semi-centralized, bureaucratic mechanisms of taxation that set the tone for the next two and a half centuries. In addition, he began the process of disarming the peasants and hence of institutionalizing the social and political divide between the samurai class and the rest of Japan. Nobunaga's successor, Toyotomi Hideyoshi, would build directly on this move by instigating a nation-wide 'sword hunt' in 1588. By the early 17th century, it became illegal for anyone other than a member of the samurai class to carry a sword; wearing two swords became the unique privilege and emblem of the samurai minority.

In an unprecedented step, Nobunaga rejected the title of shogun, which had traditionally been bestowed by the emperor since Minamoto Yoritomo received the title in 1192, inaugurating the Kamakura *bakufu*. By making this stand, Nobunaga wished to demonstrate that he was not subordinate to the emperor in Kyoto (that is, he was not the emperor's 'barbarian subduing generalissimo'), but rather that he was related directly to the land of Japan (or *tenka* – the domain under heaven) without the need for mediation by the imperial household. In other words, Nobunaga wanted Japan to acknowledge his right to rule based on a kind of *realpolitik* (that is, his *power* to rule should itself be sufficient to *legitimize* his rule), rather than on any religious or mystical endorsement by the relatively powerless imperial court. Very quickly, however, this radical possibility was closed down by Nobunaga's successors: Tokugawa Ieyasu accepted the title of shogun from the emperor in 1603 as a way to stabilize and legitimize his new regime. In the end, Pax Tokugawa did rest upon the sanction of the emperor.

Nobunaga's successor, Toyotomi Hideyoshi, was a self-made leader of men who had been in his service since about 1557. Without being high-born, Hideyoshi rapidly rose to prominence through his strategic brilliance, and he firmly consolidated the achievements of Nobunaga by building an elaborate system of alliances. By the 1590s, Hideyoshi was the undisputed master of a nation-wide federation of daimyo, each bound to him by oaths of loyalty, gratitude, debt, and fear. He administered the realm together with a group of trusted lieutenants, who kept track of the sprawling federation and the many pledged warlords. However, the successful accomplishment of this unprecedented matrix of alliances risked undermining itself, since it was premised at least partially upon the distribution of reward and punishment during war. Hideyoshi worried that the outbreak of peace threatened to cause the collapse of the loyalty system: in the absence of battle-spoils for his retainers, what was the basis of Hideyoshi's legitimacy? Unlike Nobunaga, Hideyoshi actively sought the title of shogun from the emperor to bolster his legitimacy. However, his advances were rebuffed. In a final attempt, Hideyoshi asked the deposed Ashikaga Yoshiaki (who had retained the empty title of shogun even after being driven from his court by Nobunaga) to adopt him so that he could inherit the title. Yoshiaki also refused. In the end, Hideyoshi received the title of *kampaku* (advisor to an adult emperor), which was originally held by the Fujiwara family.

We can see that Hideyoshi was engaged in the complicated and delicate politics of *power* versus *authority* that had existed between the military leaders of Japan and the imperial court for many centuries. Indeed, the problems of this political arrangement would persist under the surface of the Tokugawa Peace and would resurface violently in the events that followed the arrival of Commodore Perry in the 19th century. In some ways, as we will see later, this dynamic can be seen all the way through to the Pacific War in the first half of the 20th century. In contemporary Japan, the role and status of the emperor is legally clarified by the postwar constitution, and yet the institution (now the only emperor on the planet) is still invested with great prestige and symbolic authority over the legitimacy of the government (which is now responsible to the sovereign people, not the emperor).

In the apparent absence of the symbolic legitimacy and stability that he craved, Hideyoshi tried to mobilize the collective forces of 'Japan' by launching invasions of Korea in 1592 and 1597. It is important to realize that these invasions were not modern, national wars of the kind seen in Europe after the French Revolution, but rather they were crusades by samurai forces who expected to profit from the adventure: there was no national Japanese army, and the vast majority of the population had been systematically disarmed during the 'sword hunts'. Hideyoshi realized that the loyalty of some of the daimyo and their samurai was premised upon a flow of war-spoils. However, the invasions were disastrous. Rather than bolstering his position, the failures left his family's coffers depleted and undermined his status as an unassailable general, opening the door for the eventual ascension of Tokugawa Ieyasu. Nonetheless, Hideyoshi's abortive invasions underline the tendency for emerging states to redirect domestic discontent to overseas adventures. In the case of Japan, as we will see again at the turn of the 20th century, the first target for such expansionism has usually been Korea.

Hideyoshi's concern with the foreign was also manifested in his treatment of the Jesuit missionaries that had started to proselytize in Kyûshû in the mid-16th century. Whilst Nobunaga had been relatively accommodating of Christians, perhaps because of his opposition to the power of Buddhist temples and his dismissal of the religious importance of the emperor, Hideyoshi found the presence of these Europeans suspicious and threatening, especially following the Spanish conquest of the Philippines. In 1597, Hideyoshi turned his wrath against the Jesuits, crucifying a number of missionaries and Japanese converts before expelling the Christians from Japan in 1598. This move foreshadowed the famous *sakoku-rei* (closed-country edict) of 1635, which remained in force until the arrival of US Commodore Perry. The edict banned Catholicism as a dangerous, subversive ideology. It forbade all Japanese subjects from leaving Japan and outlawed contact with all European powers except the Dutch (in their tiny trade enclave on Deshima islet, Nagasaki). The edict also restricted contact with Japan's neighbours, at least in principle (if not in practice) limiting trade with China to passage through the island chain of the Ryûkyû Kingdom (present-day Okinawa) and with Korea to the tiny island domain of Tsushima. Whilst it would be an overstatement to say that *sakoku* completely isolated Tokugawa Japan from the outside world, it drastically reduced Japan's knowledge of Europe at precisely the moment when the Enlightenment movement began, kick-starting the development of modern science and philosophy.

After Hideyoshi's death in 1598, his lieutenants were unable to maintain stability, since the complicated system of alliances that unified Japan was tied together in the person of Hideyoshi himself. As a result, there was a fight for succession. In the end, it was Tokugawa Ieyasu who emerged supreme after the epic battle of Sekigahara in 1600, which set his own forces and those of his allies against the combined forces of his challengers, who remained loyal to the house of Toyotomi. Within three years of his victory, Ieyasu was offered the title of shogun by the emperor, and he accepted. While the emperor remained secluded in his palace in the official capital of Kyoto, the Tokugawa *bakufu* ruled a peaceful Japan from its seat of power in Edo from 1603 to 1868. Once granted by the emperor, the position of shogun became hereditary, which is why the era is named after the Tokugawa family (or sometimes after the seat of their government, Edo), and it was this government that received Commodore Perry in 1853 and 1854.

The contours of Pax Tokugawa and the genesis of modernity

The social and political contours of the Tokugawa regime were determined largely by Ieyasu and by his grandson, Iemitsu. In an attempt to end the condition of warfare that had wracked Japan for centuries, they sought to institutionalize solutions to Japan's long-standing political problems, which at that time were largely of an interpersonal and hierarchical nature: the relationship between the emperor and the shogun; the relationship between the shogun and the daimyo; the relationship between daimyo and their samurai vassals; the relationships between the samurai and the rest of the population; and hence the relationship between the population of Japan and the shogun.

The institutional solutions formulated by the Tokugawa are usually grouped under the label *bakuhan taisei*, which was ostensibly a feudal political structure linking the *bakufu* (tent/military government) with the *han* (domains ruled by daimyo) in a single *taisei* (system). However, the question of whether this system was genuinely feudal remains contested. One of the key issues in this debate, which has relevance for the modern period, concerns the dynamic between the emperor and the shogun: it is unusual for a feudal system to accommodate two separate institutional authorities at its apex – imperial authority and shogunal power. This tension was a characteristic source of instability in Japanese history.

Ieyasu resolved the tension in a very practical way: rather than merely accepting that the legitimacy of the *bakufu* was premised upon the patronage of the imperial court (hence implying the relative inferiority of his shogunate), Ieyasu made it very clear that the court was completely reliant on the *bakufu* for its very existence. This reliance went beyond the original mandate of the first shoguns (that is, to be the emperor's sword in the protection of the realm): in the early-modern world, the imperial court risked impoverishment and collapse – it actually depended upon the Tokugawa for economic support for its own subsistence.

There was no question that Ieyasu would let the imperial court vanish; instead he bought it into his service. By providing the court with funds (and leaving it in Kyoto, far away from his new government in Edo), he was able to increase its grandeur and status, but also to further emphasize its basically symbolic nature, further marginalizing it from actual power. At the same time, he could employ the emperor's reliance on the *bakufu* to bolster his own legitimacy. In return for this support, the court effectively surrendered the last vestiges of its authority, even its powers in the realm of the award of imperial honours. In many ways, the Tokugawa regime transformed the imperial house into a kind of modern, constitutional monarchy (although Japan was without a constitution until 1868, and the 1868 constitution granted the emperor far more power than he enjoyed during the Tokugawa regime).

In fact, Ieyasu was not satisfied with this surprisingly modern structure, and he took measures to give the shogunate its own religious and spiritual legitimacy, independent of (and even in competition with) that of the imperial house. He established new religious sites near Edo (such as his own shrine in Nikkô), which gradually became sites of national worship with status equal to the traditional imperial shrines, including the great shrine of Ise. Indeed, imperial officers were required to pay their respects at these Tokugawa shrines without any special privileges. Like Nobunaga before him, Ieyasu wanted his *bakufu* to be related directly to the *tenka* (realm under heaven) without the necessary mediation of the imperial house. The Tokugawa regime not only subordinated the emperor as a tool of their polity, but it also embarked on the process of building a national consciousness that did not require the emperor at all. To some extent, these two processes contradicted each other, and the Pax Tokugawa never succeeded in developing a non-imperial national consciousness; it was this failure that in turn provided an important condition of the possibility for the revolutionary turmoil of the 19th century.

Having reached a stable resolution of the question of the relationship between the emperor and shogun, the next issue concerned the relationship between the shogun and the daimyo lords. In practical terms, this was probably the most important and pressing issue after Sekigahara, since any system of government that failed to reliably incorporate (and satisfactorily placate) the warlords would be doomed. To this end, Ieyasu adopted a mixed approach of rewards and punishment, drawing in and empowering those who had demonstrated their loyalty to him at Sekigahara (the so-called *fudai daimyo*), while pushing out and disempowering those who had stood against him (the so-called *tozama daimyo*). In practice, this meant moving daimyo out of their traditional domains (and hence cutting them off from their grass-roots power bases), confiscating the lands of many lords, reallocating large tracts to the Tokugawa family itself, and giving the rest to a much smaller group of daimyo. The result was a new distribution of about 180 daimyo, each of whom had sworn an oath of loyalty to the Tokugawa. These daimyo were forbidden from establishing more than one castle per domain, and they were also forbidden from forming alliances with each other; on a formal level (even if not in practice) they related to each other only through the national institution of the shogunate. The *fudai daimyo* were lords of the domains closest to Edo and Tokugawa lands, while the *tozama daimyo* tended to be focused around the periphery, such as in the outlying lands of Satsuma and Chôshû.

In this way, Ieyasu protected himself, but this was at the cost of the ability to closely monitor those daimyo who were most likely to resent his power. In an unfortunate combination of factors, these were also the domains most likely to encounter (and trade with) foreign powers. Despite his attempts, Hideyoshi had not managed to eradicate all the Christians in Kyûshû, and Iemitsu's *sakoku-rei* did not cut off all contact with the outside world. By the 19th century, Satsuma and Chôshû in particular would greatly increase their power in Japan through their relative openness to learning from overseas.

In practice, this process of centralization was weak, which was partly a deliberate ploy to reduce opposition to the centralization process, but it was also because the levels of centralization typical of a modern nation-state were as yet unthinkable in Japan. Importantly, the regional domains retained a high degree of fiscal autonomy: although daimyo were obliged to make contributions to public works and other costs, there was no consistent or centralized tax regime. Hence, wealth disparities around the realm were significant. However, the Tokugawa regime imposed one extremely important financial (and strategic) burden on all the daimyo. In the late 1630s, Tokugawa Iemitsu implemented the *sankin kôtai* system of 'alternate attendance', which obliged every daimyo in Japan to maintain residences in Edo as well as in their home domains. Furthermore, daimyo were actually required to reside in Edo every other year, and their immediate family had to stay there permanently. Although their conditions were good, the family of daimyo were effectively hostages in Edo.

The *sankin kôtai* system had a number of important effects on the development of modern Japan. In the first instance, the requirement to maintain two major residences, often at great distances apart, combined with the requirement to 'process' with full entourage from one to the other every year, acted as a severe drain on the coffers of the daimyo, effectively checking the growth of their autonomous power. In addition, the hostage system discouraged dissident daimyo from moving against the Tokugawa, even if they could afford it. The stabilizing influence of these factors should not be underestimated, especially in the early years of the Tokugawa period when the legacy of centuries of warfare was still relatively fresh in the minds of some of the warlords. In the long term, however, the financial impact of this arrangement would cause great social and political tension, which would contribute to the decline of the Tokugawa regime even before the arrival of Perry.

Another vital consequence of *sankin kôtai* was the way that it encouraged the development of a sense of 'nation', perhaps for the first time in Japan. All the daimyo, no matter where they were from and no matter what their beliefs, had to spend half of their time in Edo – consolidating the status of that city as the effective capital of Japan (even while Kyoto continued to hold that distinction in theory). And they were obliged to do so by a *national law*. Hence, *sankin kôtai* not only encouraged daimyo and their retinues to identify with a national unit of organization, but it also reinforced the fact that the central authority in that unit was the secular institution of the *bakufu* rather than the traditional and sacred authority of the imperial house. In addition, being away from their home domains for 50% of their time greatly reduced the affinities between the daimyo and their traditional local support networks. Daimyo – the *regional* lords – gradually became *national* figures.

An important side-effect of the *sankin kôtai* system was that it riddled the fragmented country with transport routes and trading possibilities. The yearly processions of daimyo and their retainers threaded together the economies of the domains through which they passed, resulting in the rapid growth of market towns and trading stations as well as the development of one of the most impressive road networks in the world. Most spectacular of these successes was the explosive growth of Osaka along the famous Tôkaidô highway that linked Kyoto to Edo, as well as the construction of the Nakasendô highway through the Japan Alps. In a very real sense, the *sankin kôtai* system kick-started the development of a national market economy that saw dramatic growth through the 17th century and laid the foundations for rapid economic modernization in the 19th century.

The geographical mobility encouraged by the system of alternate attendance also began a process of urbanization. By the end of the 17th century, Edo was the largest city on the planet, with a population in excess of one million. Present-day Tokyo remains one of the world's largest cities, with a metropolitan population of over 35 million. The provincial cities of Kyoto and Osaka were about the same size as London or Paris at that time, with about 350,000 people. Osaka remains Japan's second largest city in the present day. Overall, about 10% of the Japanese population lived in cities of a substantial size at the end of the 17th century, making it one of the most urbanized countries in the world. Not only that: fuelled by a new social stability (and the end of constant warfare), increasing domestic trade, increasing literacy, and advances in farming techniques, Japan's population actually doubled during the 17th century, reaching approximately 33 million by the turn of the 18th century. By comparison, at that time the population of Britain was about 5 million, and it would not reach 30 million until the second half of the 19th century.

This level of growth was unsustainable in Japan, at least partly because the domestic market was severely hampered by the islands' poor natural resources, and especially by the fact that the *bakufu* had isolated itself from open trade with continental Asia, let alone with Europe. The result was economic and demographic stagnation, and there was zero growth for the last century of the Tokugawa period. Hence, by the time of the second arrival of the West, as part of the so-called second stage of globalization, Japan had developed little more than the seeds of capitalism and, despite its great cultural and artistic achievements, it was basically an economic backwater in the 19th century. In fact, the 18th and early 19th centuries witnessed mass famines, rising rates of infanticide, and increasing social unrest: Japan was teetering on the brink of crisis and revolution even before the arrival of Perry. In contrast, in the same period Britain's population had soared to match that of Japan, and its industrial, imperial economy spanned the globe hungrily.

An increasingly nationalized sense of space, and thus a new degree of geographical mobility, was not matched by social mobility between classes in Tokugawa Japan. Indeed, one of the most powerful features of Tokugawa society was the establishment of the so-called *shi-nô-kô-shô* system of stratification that determined the status and functions of the vast majority of the population, as well as their relationships with the daimyo. This four-tiered structure enshrined the samurai (*shi*) at the top of the hierarchy, with farmers (*nô*) next in terms of status, then artisans (*kô*), and finally merchants (*shô*) at the bottom. One's place in this hierarchical system was determined by birth, and mobility thereafter was extremely difficult if not impossible. The system was justified in Confucian terms by the Tokugawa regime's formative ideologues, such as the neo-Confucian Hayashi Razan.

Confucian principles emphasized the importance of piety and loyalty, and in particular the proper designation of roles within society. The ruler and the ruled stood in a rational and natural relation to each other, just as heaven reached over earth, or as a father ruled over his son and the son owed filial piety to his father. These relationships were held to be inalienable parts of the natural order, and thus not open to being challenged by the will of man. In the context of the fledgling Tokugawa regime, this appeal to stability was very useful, and it helped to justify the rigidity and lack of social mobility in the *shi-nô-kô-shô* system. In particular, Hayashi Razan would argue that the loyalty of the people was owed to the shogun (rather than to the emperor, whom he depoliticized), effectively rendering the shogun as the father of the nation. In other words, the Tokugawa regime utilized a nationalized and rational model of political obligation – on the world stage, it was one of the most 'modern' societies of the time.

The so-called 'Tokugawa ideology' also drew elements from Buddhism. Indeed, after Hideyoshi had broken the back of the military power of a number of Buddhist temples at the close of the 16th century, Tokugawa Ieyasu and then Iemitsu brought the Buddhist establishment back into the fold by obliging all commoners in the land to register with a Buddhist temple. Tokugawa patronage of Buddhism was, perhaps unintentionally, a way of off-setting the sacred position of the emperor in the religion of Shintô, the indigenous religion of Japan, which finds its textual roots in the *Kojiki* (c. 712), according to which the emperor is a direct descendant of the Sun-Goddess, Amaterasu-ômikami, and hence should be revered as a living god. From the point of view of the social order, however, Buddhism (and especially Zen Buddhism) had another role to play: through the influence of thinkers such as Suzuki Shôsan, principles of stoicism and non-discrimination promoted stability and discouraged dissent and resistance within the *shi-nô-kô-shô* system. In particular, Zen became very popular amongst the samurai, who found themselves without a military role in Japanese society for the first time in centuries. Indeed, the close association of Zen with the samurai that is so commonplace in present-day novels and movies is really premised on the way in which samurai turned to this religion after the outbreak of peace; samurai-zen was never really a feature of the earlier *sengoku-jidai* when the samurai were at war.

By the 18th century, however, the Tokugawa social system was beginning to become a victim of its own success. Stability began to look like sterility, and the problem of how to accommodate and even encourage social *change* became very important. In particular, as the economy faltered, social commentators began to notice the increasing poverty and suffering in both the cities and rural areas. The emerging cities were unhygienic and the countryside was speckled with famine and starvation, where the toil of the farmers (who represented 80% of the population) only seemed to increase. Meanwhile, the emerging merchant class was gradually becoming wealthier, despite its ostensible position at the bottom of the social hierarchy. At the same time, the samurai, who were basically cost-centres in the Tokugawa system, were bleeding their traditional financial means; despite being at the top of the status system, they were rapidly losing the affluence required to demonstrate it. In addition, without war to demonstrate their worth (and their alleged stoic values), the samurai were losing the respect of the rest of the population. Because the status of samurai was determined based on heredity (about 6% of the population) rather than merit, resentment about incompetence was increasingly widespread, until 'the ability of a samurai' actually became an insulting phrase. This process was exacerbated by the apparent duplicity of the samurai, who frowned upon the mercantile values of the emerging urban classes, but who were themselves the most ostentatious patrons of the so-called *ukiyo* (floating world) – the rapidly growing pleasure districts in the cities. Ironically, the patronage of the samurai helped to fuel a tremendous explosion in artistic development: some of the most famous art forms of early-modern Japan find their origins in this period, especially *ukiyoe* (pictures of the floating world) and *kabuki* theatre, with the latter serving a double function as the home of actresses qua courtesans. The denizens of the *ukiyo* were technically outside the *shi-nô-kô-shô* system, since they represented new commercial and artistic occupations that could not easily be placed into one of the traditional categories. These pleasure districts remain colourful parts of Japan's major cities to this day, and the cult of celebrity is more powerful than ever in contemporary Japan.

For some contemporary commentators, such as the famous political theorist Maruyama Masao, the difficult circumstances of the 18th century actually provided the ground for the seeds of a Japanese modernity to be sown. Maruyama and others point in particular to the work of Ogyû Sorai, a pioneer of so-called *kogaku* (ancient learning). Sorai represented a serious challenge to the neo-Confucian orthodoxy, albeit from within a Confucian framework. He agreed that the basis of correct thinking and conduct could be found in the ancient Chinese classics, but he argued that clinging to the letter of these texts in a static or conservative manner was a mistake. He argued that it was the historical function of great leaders to interpret and adjust the implementation of these texts, based on sound scholarship into the original texts but also based on the particular circumstances of the present. In other words, Sorai argued that even a Confucian political system should be dynamic and adaptable to the changing needs of society, and that clinging to the past simply for the sake of maintaining a previously stable model was morally wrong. Whilst it would be quite wrong to suggest that Sorai was calling for the *bakufu* to become a responsible and responsive modern government respecting the social and political rights of the population of Japan, some historians have maintained that his arguments prepared the ground for these developments in the modern period.

A particular target of Sorai's critique was the persistence of what he considered to be anachronistic social practices, such as the pompous attitudes of the samurai towards the rising merchant class. Indeed, the role of the samurai in Tokugawa society was a central concern, since the continuing existence of their class was increasingly difficult to rationalize. A straw in the wind after 1702 was the so-called Akô Incident, otherwise known as the revenge of the 47 *rônin* (masterless samurai). In this famous story, which is now a national legend in Japan, 47 samurai avenged the death of their daimyo master (the Lord of Akô) after he was forced to commit *seppuku* (suicide by self disembowelment – also known more vulgarly as *hara-kiri*, or cutting the stomach). Despite the fact that the Tokugawa regime had strictly banned vendetta killings, the loyal samurai plotted their revenge for 22 months, knowing that they would meet their own deaths whether or not their plot succeeded. Eventually, the *rônin* executed their plan and assassinated the daimyo responsible for the death of their lord. They then turned themselves in to the authorities and voluntarily performed *seppuku* as punishment for their crime.

This case caused a great deal of controversy at the time, and it has remained an important part of Japan's national identity into the modern period. For Sorai, no matter what the chivalrous merits of the 47 *rônin*, their actions betrayed an anachronistic sense of loyalty to one's daimyo rather than to the laws of the land. The 47 *rônin* were icons of a pre-national age, and they demonstrated how the traditional values of the samurai class might be an obstacle to the modernization of Japan. However, for other sections of the population (including various other samurai), the actions of these *rônin* represented the ideals of *bushidô* (the way of the warrior) and demonstrated that the traditional values of loyalty, sacrifice, endurance, and honour had not been eradicated by the Tokugawa Peace. Indeed, the Akô Incident quickly became one of the most popular topics in Japanese culture, inspiring *kabuki* and *bunraku* playwrights as well as artists until the present day. Arguably Japan's greatest playwright, Chikamatsu, wrote the most famous version of the play, *Chûshingura*, and Japan's greatest *ukiyo-e* artists all produced picture series based on the story: Hiroshige, Hokusai, Kunisada, and of course Kuniyoshi. In contemporary culture, there

5. *Rônin* dressed as police, shown in a scene from the play *Chûshingura*, woodcut, *c.*1804–12

are movies, novels, manga (graphic fiction), anime, and even video games devoted to the legend, and the graves of the *rônin* have become major tourist attractions.

In other words, the tension between traditional and new social values that is commonly associated with the process of modernization was already an important feature of Tokugawa society at the start of the 18th century. Romantic images of the samurai as stoic, honourable retainers willing to lay down their lives for the sake of their lords became the stuff of popular culture, not only for the consumption of the masses but also for the samurai themselves. But these ideals stood in stark contrast to the actual experience of life in Tokugawa Japan: most samurai had never drawn their blades in combat; vendettas were banned; loyalty was expected to be focused on the shogun and the *tenka* rather than local lords; urban samurai were increasingly decadent consumers, while rural samurai rapidly lost their status. For many, the samurai were a burden rather than an icon of society. Ironically, then, while the Akô Incident risked undermining the social order for a brief moment, in practice it quickly became an important element in the construction of a modern national consciousness.

Bakumatsu and the Meiji Restoration

So, when Commodore Perry arrived, Japan was a complicated and conflict-ridden society. It had many of the features of a modern nation, with a nation-wide state apparatus under the secular control of the *bakufu* in Edo, which in turn relied on the religious authority of the imperial house in Kyoto for part of its legitimacy. After centuries of peace and relative stability, Japan had a sophisticated domestic market economy, albeit one that remained partially outside the regional, Asian system. Its national culture was blossoming, especially in the large, well-organized cities of Edo and Osaka. However, the ideological and economic foundations of the regime were crumbling, and social tensions simmered between the classes in the anachronistic and rigid stratification system. The *bakufu* had no centralized or coherent taxation system, no system of national mobilization of force, and only limited ability to control the relations of the semi-autonomous domains with the outside world. In other words, Perry found a nation in the throws of a process of modernization that had been frustrated from the outset by a polity deliberately designed to promote stasis and stability – a polity on the point of revolution. Historians have labelled the period between 1853 and 1868 the *bakumatsu* – the end of the shogunate.

Perry's arrival acted as a catalyst in the volatile mix, triggering and framing a series of events that finally culminated in the overthrow of the *bakufu* and the installation of the emperor as the sovereign of a modern, constitutional state. After over two centuries of carefully cultivating its political supremacy in Japan and of isolating the imperial court as a symbolic functionary, perhaps the most inexplicable acts in this series of events were orchestrated by the *bakufu* itself: first, after Perry's first visit in 1853, the chief councillor of the *bakufu*, Abe Masahiro, took the unprecedented step of asking the daimyo for their views on how to respond to Perry's ultimatum. Whilst his intention may have been to build a national consensus, which was certainly important in the face of the threat, the effect was rather to suggest that the *bakufu* lacked the necessary powers of leadership at this critical moment. The result, in fact, was that Abe was forced to resign. There was no consensus, and a powerful faction of anti-foreign daimyo emerged onto the national stage, already talking about the potential role of the emperor as a stronger national leader at such a time of unprecedented crisis.

The second event was even more astonishing: after Perry's return and the installation of Townsend Harris as US Consul in Shimoda, discussion turned to the matter of a trade agreement. At that time, the shogun, Tokugawa Iesada, was sick and dying, and the question of his succession was also in the air. Abe's successor, Hotta Masayoshi, had the difficult job of negotiating solutions to these twin problems. Together with the daimyo of the *fudai* domains, Hotta wanted to accept Harris's trade agreement and also to appoint the malleable 12-year-old Tokugawa Iemochi, heir to the domain of Kii – a Tokugawa branch family. Unfortunately, buoyed by the apparent weakness of the *bakufu* at this difficult time, the *tozama* daimyo (most notably Satsuma), together with some other anti-foreign domains (such as Mito, which was actually a branch of the Tokugawa family), held the opposite opinions on both issues, wanting to reject the treaty and to appoint Tokugawa Yoshinobu (the son of the powerful Mito daimyo, Tokugawa Nariaki).

In response to the conflict, Hotta took the astonishing step of travelling to Kyoto to ask Emperor Kômei to ratify Harris's treaty and to confirm the *bakufu's* choice of shogunal hier. For the first time in centuries, the emperor was drawn into the heart of political decision-making. Unfortunately for Hotta, the emperor turned out to have outspoken anti-foreign views, and to be a supporter of Tokugawa Yoshinobu; the increasingly imperialist daimyo of Satsuma and Mito had already been at Kômei's ear. Humiliated, Hotta returned to Edo having radically undermined the legitimacy of the Tokugawa *bakufu*, and with a directive from the emperor that contradicted the wishes of the shogunate. He resigned.

Despite a crackdown by Ii Naosuke, Hotta's successor, the damage to the legitimacy of the *bakufu* had already been done, and it was not possible to get the genie back into the bottle. Ii's uncompromising actions against the radical daimyo succeeded only in further alienating the anti-foreign factions, pushing them further towards an anti-*bakufu* and pro-imperial position. Within two years, a group of samurai from the Mito domain had assassinated Ii in the heart of Edo, and thereafter the *bakufu* was intimidated into being as accommodating as possible. In 1862, for instance, the shogun finally cancelled *sankin kôtai* and requested the daimyo to use the money they saved to contribute to the defence of the nation by building up their own regional military forces. Whilst this may have been intended as an accommodation, the effect was to politically decentralize Edo, to remove one of the heaviest financial burdens on the restive daimyo, and simultaneously to actually encourage these daimyo to build powerful private armies. Tokugawa's pretence of national unity was crumbling.

By the 1860s, then, the *bakufu* was under threat from three different directions at once. First, there was the challenge to its rule from the increasingly discontented and increasingly unrestrained *tozama* daimyo. Second, there was a genuine risk of social uprising from young samurai, or *shishi* (men of purpose), who called themselves 'loyalists' because they aimed to reinstate direct imperial rule in Japan, believing that the *bakufu* had illegitimately usurped the emperor's position. In practice, these *shishi* tended to be found in the *tozama* domains, especially in Satsuma and Chôshû, although some could be found in more central areas such as Mito. They rallied under the slogan *sonnô jôi* (revere the emperor and repel the barbarians), but under the leadership of samurai intellectuals such as Yoshida Shôin (from Chôshû) and Sakamoto Ryôma (from Tosa) the *shishi* were increasingly pragmatic in their view of the West, seeing in Western technology the promise of sufficient power to overthrow the *bakufu* and also to keep the West at bay. The third threat to the *bakufu* came from outside Japan: the pressure being exerted by the Western powers. However, in many ways, this external pressure was really part of the context for the other two challenges, rather than a challenge in itself.

Under the influence of the radicalized atmosphere in Kyoto, Emperor Kômei himself started to reassert the authority of the imperial house. In 1862, he issued an official request to the shogun, as his 'barbarian-subduing generalissimo', to expel the Western barbarians from Japan, setting a deadline of 25 June 1863. When the deadline passed, the *bakufu* made no attempt to affect the expulsion. However, in other parts of Japan anti-*bakufu* 'loyalists' were agitating. Samurai in Chôshû, who had industriously armed themselves with Western firearms, actually opened fire on an American ship off the coast. Retaliation was swift and violent. One of the results was that the Chôshû domain became a magnet for radicals and loyalists; the next year they formed an army and marched towards Kyoto, aiming to 'liberate' the emperor from the *bakufu*'s control.

Through the brokerage of the Tosa samurai, Sakamoto Ryôma, the *tozama* domains of Chôshû and Satsuma began to realize that they shared a great deal in common. Not only did they have long-standing grievances against the Tokugawa, but they also contained a unusually high proportion of samurai (up to 25%), and these samurai tended towards 'loyalist' principles. Furthermore, these outlying domains had exploited the fact that they were distant from Edo by carefully and enthusiastically cultivating knowledge of the West and of modern technology since the arrival of Perry. By the mid-1860s, they were rapidly developing modern military forces that were at least the equal of the *bakufu*'s army. Even more progressively, Chôshû samurai such as Takashugi Shinsaku were devising military units that incorporated non-samurai, effectively ending the 250-year-ban on non-samurai bearing arms. Indeed, Takashugi's militia was perhaps Japan's first modern, 'popular' army.

In 1866, Chôshû and Satsuma agreed a fateful, secret (and illegal) alliance. In the same year, Tokugawa Iemochi died of a heart condition, and the new Shogun, Tokugawa Yoshinobu of Mito, decided to launch a campaign against Chôshû to punish it for its misadventures and to make an example of it. Yoshinobu was also a modernizer, and the *bakufu* was receiving considerable assistance from the USA and France to build a modern military. Nonetheless, when the *bakufu* forces neared Chôshû in the far southwest of the country, Satsuma unexpectedly refused its call for support. As a result, the *bakufu* army was defeated by Chôshû and was forced to embark on a humiliating retreat back through the entire length of Japan to Edo. For the first time in centuries, the *bakufu* was shown to be militarily inadequate to the task of controlling the realm; its last and most basic claim to legitimacy was destroyed. In the following months, there was an explosion of social unrest and peasant uprisings across the nation, reflecting the crisis of legitimacy that was exacerbated by the sight of the defeated *bakufu* army marching home, and also by the omen of change represented by the death of Emperor Kômei in 1867. Kômei's son, Emperor Meiji, took the throne in February 1867.

In the aftermath of the *bakufu*'s defeat, Tosa again tried to play the intermediary, convincing Shogun Yoshinobu to accept the need for wholesale political reform, the establishment of a Prussian-style parliament and the reversion of sovereignty to the emperor. Indeed, Yoshinobu appears to have agreed to these reforms. However, it was already too late for the *bakufu*: the daimyo of Satsuma and Chôshû had decided to capitalize on the opportunity to take matters into their own hands. In an audacious step in December 1867, the combined armies of the two domains marched on Kyoto, occupied the city, and took control of the imperial palace. Within a month, they had convinced the new Emperor Meiji to pronounce an imperial restoration, effectively abolishing the *bakufu* by imperial decree in January 1868.

Shogun Yoshinobu resisted the decree, and thus began a bloody conflict that has come to be known as the Boshin War. In fact, the war was effectively over within months, as Yoshinobu's attack on Kyoto was repelled easily and he was forced to retreat back to Edo. Edo itself fell in April 1868, when Yoshinobu's legendary commander, Katsu Kaishû, handed the city over to the imperial forces without resistance, apparently because he thought that unity and peace were more important than the preservation of the *bakufu*. Thus was affected the Meiji Restoration: a modern revolution, with modernized, mass armies using Western firearms and guided by European strategic thinking.

Chapter 2
Imperial revolution: embracing modernity

Emperor Meiji processed triumphantly from the ancient capital of Kyoto to Edo in 1868, and within a year his temporary palace in the eastern city was declared the new Imperial Palace. At that moment, Edo officially became the new capital of Japan, Tokyo – the Capital of the East. For the insurgents as well as for *bakufu* loyalists, this Imperial Restoration was dramatic and bloody, and expectations of change in the capital were high. However, for the vast majority of the population of Japan, the Meiji Restoration (if they had noticed it at all) was little more than a samurai rebellion or *coup d'état*. Indeed, the people of Japan had very little reason to be optimistic that their living conditions would improve markedly, and they had every right to be sceptical that the drama of the last decades would result simply in another reshuffling of power and privilege amongst the samurai class.

However, there were a number of very important differences between the 17th- and the 19th-century political revolutions, and over the next decade Japan was genuinely transformed. Even if the bloody events of 1868 should be considered an elite movement, the Meiji Restoration became a genuine revolution in the period between 1868 and the early 1880s: Japanese society and the conditions of life at every level of it were profoundly transformed.

The tone for these changes was set just after the establishment of the emperor in Edo, when he promulgated the so-called Charter Oath (sometimes called the Five-Article Oath), in which the new government (in the name of the emperor) made five radical pledges:

1) to establish deliberative assemblies in order to involve the public in decision-making;
2) to involve all levels of society 'from the highest to the lowest' in the affairs of the state;
3) to abolish restrictions on the occupation and function for all the people;
4) to abandon the superstitions of the past and to embrace rational laws of nature;
5) to seek knowledge from around the world to strengthen Japan.

These pledges represented the complete dismantling of the *bakuhan taisei*, and the apparent embrace of a number of principles of modern governance. Aside from the imperialist impulse within Japan and the drive to construct a powerful nation, the adoption of a modern political system was itself one of the explicit goals of the reforms; the revolutionary government was critically aware that the only way they could free Japan from the humiliation of the Unequal Treaties was to create a political system that the Western powers could respect as equal to their own.

The new government tried again and again to have the treaties revoked, but it was repeatedly frustrated by the foreign powers, who insisted that they would not give up their privileges before the legal and political system of Japan could provide adequately 'modern' protection of their rights. Here, 'modern' and 'civilized' were used in the same breath. In the end, after riots, protests, and wholesale reform in Japan, the treaties were renegotiated in the 1890s. By which time Japan had a national currency, a national taxation system, a bicameral legislature, and a formal constitution that protected the rights and duties of the Japanese and established the rule of law, albeit in a qualified sense. In addition, in the 'Age of Empires', Japan's identity as a fledgling imperial power was already evident: the new regime assimilated the northern island of Hokkaido in 1869 and the southern kingdom of Okinawa in 1879; it had made plans for an invasion of Korea as early as 1873; and by 1895, it had already employed its newly modernized military to defeat its giant neighbour, China, in its first major war of the modern period, taking Taiwan as part of the spoils. In other words, by the 1890s, Japan had begun to present itself as the first modernized Asian power, under the slogan *fukoku kyôhei* (rich country, strong army).

In sum, the reforms in the wake of the Restoration had both domestic and international impetuses. The powerful external pressure on the new regime was one of the critical factors that set the project of state formation during Meiji apart from the earlier project of nation formation during Tokugawa; the power and menace of the so-called 'second phase' of Western globalization that carried the full force of capitalist expansionism was irresistible. Modern Japan's uneasy relationships with its own history and traditions on the one hand, and with modernity and the West on the other, are two of the key characteristics of this period. In many ways, this is the period in which Japan sought to square this circle and forge its own modernity in the face of the industrial expansion of the West.

Symbolic reform of the Meiji state

For much of the Meiji period, particularly in the time before the promulgation of the Constitution of the Empire of Japan in 1889, the business of governance was conducted by a group of senior statesmen from the powerful domains of Satsuma, Chôshû, Tosa, and Hizen. This group, which enjoyed privileged access to the imperial house after supporting it so strongly during the

Restoration, would become known as the Satchô clique, or sometimes as the *genrô*. The effective concentration of power in the hands of a relatively small group of *tozama* daimyo represented a radical shift in the domestic balance of power, and it was met with serious resistance in some areas. One such area was the domain of Aizu, where loyalists to the Tokugawa *bakufu* continued to fight against the new imperial forces for several months after the official Restoration.

The Aizu incident provided an early indication that the Meiji regime would face some residual problems of legitimacy, despite the imperial nature of the Restoration. Hence, Emperor Meiji established a new, national shrine in Tokyo, the *Tokyo shôkonsha*, which would become the official resting place of the spirits (*kami*) of all soldiers who died in the name of imperial Japan. This move echoed the nation-building symbolism of the shrines at Nikkô that were built by the Tokugawa in order to de-privilege the imperial shrine at Ise and provide a new focus for national worship; establishing a national religious icon to legitimate a new regime is a feature of Japanese history.

In 1879, Meiji's new shrine was renamed *Yasukuni jinja* (the name that it retains to this day), and it would become a central edifice in the emerging state Shintô religion, which the new regime encouraged as a means of legitimizing the Imperial Restoration. Significantly for the symbolism of the new Japan, the Aizu and other pro-Tokugawa forces were not enshrined in Yasukuni, indicating that they were enemies of the emperor and the state – a charge that still causes controversy today. It was not until after the Pacific War (in 1965) that a new *chinreisha* (or spirit-pacifying shrine) was built within the Yasukuni compound to honour the souls of those who had died in Japan's civil wars since 1853. This represented a deliberate attempt to help create a more inclusive sense of nation for postwar society.

The most famous *kami* enshrined in the *chinreisha* belong to the near-legendary samurai from Hizen and Satsuma, Etô Shimpei and Saigô Takamori, who led the Saga Rebellion (1874) and the Satsuma Rebellion (1877) against the Meiji government even after being so instrumental in establishing it, claiming that it had betrayed the true spirit of Japan: invoking the traditions of the samurai, they killed themselves to evade capture.

In other words, dissent against the ideals and policies of the Meiji regime not only lingered in the former *fudai han*, but it also emerged within the ranks of the newly empowered domains of Satsuma, Chôshû (where there was a rebellion in 1876) and elsewhere. In the contemporary period, the *chinreisha* is fenced off from the rest of the compound and guarded, after ultra-nationalist groups threatened to blow it up as an offence to the nation.

Yasukuni remains one of the most controversial institutions in modern Japan; in the second half of the 20th century, politicians have touched off public controversy in East Asia by visiting the shrine, which now also commemorates the soldiers who died in the name of the emperor during the Pacific War. For some critics, these visits indicate that contemporary Japan has failed to properly express remorse for the aggression of the Imperial Army in Asia during the 1930s and early 1940s. For others, these visits actually show a lack of respect for those who died for Imperial Japan, because the establishment of the *chinreisha* honours domestic 'enemies of the state' and even foreign soldiers who died in battle against Imperial Japan (despite the fact that it is hidden from view and largely unknown). For other commentators, these visits merely indicate a healthy sense of patriotism and respect for the history of modern Japan. The controversy shows little sign of abating today.

6. Statue of Saigo Takamori walking his dog, in Ueno Park, Tokyo

Ideological and legal reform of the Meiji state

The emperor's Charter Oath of 1868 made a number of demands on the new regime. Perhaps the easiest of them was the injunction to seek knowledge from around the world in order to modernize and strengthen Japan. This particular command had two serious implications for the new regime: a dramatic reversal of the official policy of *sakoku* that had characterized the Tokugawa regime; and a profound undermining of the neo-Confucian ideology that had characterized educational prerogatives over the last three centuries.

In practice, Japan had not been completely isolated during the period of *sakoku*, and the *bakufu* itself had sent missions to the USA (1860) and Europe (1862, 1863), but perhaps the most famous and important response to this decree was the Iwakura Embassy of 1871–3. The Iwakura mission was led by the nobleman Iwakura Tomomi; he was supported by a group of *genrô*, which included the Chôshû statesman Kido Kôin (sometimes known as Kido Takayoshi) as well as the future first prime minister of Japan, Itô Hirobumi, also from Chôshû domain. The two-year embassy travelled to the USA and then to Europe, where it visited Britain, France, the Netherlands, Russia, Germany, and other nations.

The embassy had a dual purpose: the first was to attempt to renegotiate the Unequal Treaties with the USA and the European powers; and the second was to gather knowledge about science, technology, and medicine in order to help Japan to 'catch up' with the modern Great Powers, but also to learn about modern economic, political, and legal systems. In practice, these two goals turned out to be intricately linked, since the Western nations uniformly refused to renegotiate the treaties until such a time as Japan had successfully modernized.

The mission returned to a Japan hungry for knowledge of Europe, with a fledgling civil society providing a public sphere for discourse about social, cultural, and political affairs. In the early 1870s, Japan saw the publication of its first modern newspapers, beginning in 1871 with the *Yokohama Mainichi Shinbun* and followed quickly by the *Nichinichi News* in Tokyo (the forerunner of today's *Mainichi Shinbun*). The progressive *Asahi Shinbun* also began life in this period (in Osaka, 1879). At the same time, the publishing industry started to boom, selling printed books, essays, and translations of Western books in the cities of Japan. This provided an avenue for European philosophy and literature to enter Japanese culture, and intellectuals quickly grasped the importance and potentials of these cultural imports.

A key group of progressive intellectuals in this period was known as the *Meiroku* society (the Meiji Six – so called because the group was founded in the sixth year of the Meiji period). The founders of this society included influential public intellectuals and statesmen, such as Mori Arinori, Fukuzawa Yukichi, Katô Hiroyuki, and Nishi Amane. The group, which has come to be seen as the vanguard of the so-called Japanese Enlightenment, since it embraced the ideals of the European Enlightenment that underpinned modernity in the West, published an influential magazine, *Meiroku zasshi*. The pages of the journal discussed the most pressing social and political issues of the day, such as the merits of popularly elected assemblies, the importance of the separation of religion and politics, and the place of women in society. But it also included discussions of other 'modern' topics, such as economic policy and innovations in European chemistry and physics.

Although the *Meirokusha* included a wide range of influential thinkers, perhaps the most important was the 'enlighteneer' Fukuzawa Yukichi, who had travelled to the USA in 1860 as part of a *bakufu* expedition, and then to Europe in 1862. Fukuzawa became famous after his return from Europe for his best-selling, ten-volume account of the *Conditions in the West* (*Seiyô jijô*, 1867–70), in which he showcased the achievements of Western modernity. Soon afterwards, worried about Japan's survival in the modern world, Fukuzawa wrote a series of books called *An Encouragement of Learning* (*Gakumon no susume*, 1872–6), in which he called on the Japanese to abandon their traditional (Confucian) approach to knowledge and social organization. He debunked principles of heredity and superstition, and argued strongly that society should be based on equality of opportunity and that people (no matter what their backgrounds) should find their place in society based on merit and, in particular, based on their educational achievement. Indeed, Fukuzawa was an educational pioneer: he established *Keiô gijuku* in 1858 as a means of training the youth in 'Western' knowledge; this academy was the forefather of Keiô University – Japan's first and still most prestigious private university.

Fukuzawa and the other 'enlighteneers' were part of a progressive movement in the Meiji period that rallied behind slogans such as 'civilization and enlightenment' (*bunmei kaika*), which initially equated the notion of a rational enlightenment on the European model with the attainment of civilization itself (a notion that lay close to the heart of the imperialist powers of the West, with their various, self-proclaimed 'civilizing missions'). The basic idea was that Japan needed to 'catch up' with the West in order to survive in the modern system of international relations. For a number of intellectuals and policy-makers, the logic of the international system was governed by the idea that the 'strong eat the weak' (*jakuniku kyôshoku*). This Social Darwinian idea, which Fukuzawa and others drew from the work of Herbert Spencer, became very influential in Japan and drove the nation to ever greater levels of industry and eventually imperialism.

Just as Fukuzawa's ideas about the dignity of the individual radically undermined Confucian traditions and laid the groundwork for the development of liberal ideologies in Japan, so his ideas about international relations helped to explode the traditional, China-centric view of the regional order (which placed an isolated Japan on the periphery) and to provide the conditions of the possibility for Japan to surpass China and even surpass the power and status of the Western nations. If Spencer was right about the course of history, then it followed that Europe was simply the most advanced civilization *at that point in time*, which meant that Japan could become *more advanced* and *more civilized* in the future. For Fukuzawa and various others in the decades to come, the key to surpassing the West lay in Japan's ability to assimilate 'Western technology' but to retain its own 'Eastern spirit' (*wakon yôsai*). In the next chapter, we will see that this kind of logic will feed into the call to 'overcome modernity' and indeed to 'overcome the West' in the 1930s and 1940s.

Thanks to improving education, rising literacy rates, and increasing print circulation, especially in the growing urban centres, these new and modern ideas made a real impact on the people of Japan. The 1870s and 1880s saw rapid growth in the formation of political organizations in the cities but also in rural communities. At first these groups consisted largely of samurai, but they gradually became of mixed participation. By 1881, Japan had its first national political party, the Liberal Party (*Jiyûtô*). This was followed quickly in 1882 by the Progressive Party (*Kaishintô*), led by the future prime minister, Ôkuma Shigenobu, who also founded the *Tokyo Senmon Gakkô* in the same year; the school would change its name to Waseda University in 1902, becoming Keiô's great rival to this very day.

Although these parties collapsed in 1884, they were very active in organizing petitions and rallies, in publishing manifestos and journals, and even in collecting fees from their members. In other words, they established the practice of popular politics in modern Japan. A key issue during the 1880s was the popular rights movement, which gradually garnered widespread support throughout different sectors of the population. Significantly, however, the popular rights movement never really extended to include women, despite the courageous actions and the example of a number of independently minded individuals, such as the remarkable Tsuda Umeko, who returned to Japan in 1882 after travelling to the USA with the Iwakura Embassy and established an important college for women that became Tsuda University.

For some historians, the promulgation of the Meiji Constitution in 1889 seemed like the natural result of this revolutionary groundswell of popular involvement in politics. Indeed, the new constitution did establish many of the things for which the parties had been calling. It included: a bicameral legislature with an elected lower house and an appointed upper house of peers; it guaranteed a range of rights and duties. But the constitution was formally a gift from the emperor, who retained sovereignty and who resided beyond the terms of the constitution, and the parliament was basically an advisory body.

In reality, then, it might be better to view the constitution as a strategic move by the *genrô* to prevent popular involvement in politics from getting out of hand. Indeed, the aristocratic *genrô* were deeply distrustful of the political parties and seemed to feel great disdain for the common people of Japan, believing that they were uneducated and incapable of acting for the public good rather than out of self-interest. To them, the party system seemed to indulge self-serving and fragmentary policies, which Japan could ill-afford: Japan needed to be united if it was going to 'catch up' with the West and become strong enough to survive in the volatile international system.

In other words, the promulgation of the Meiji Constitution should be seen as a way for the *genrô* to control the emergence of the people into modern political consciousness. In practice, the constitution granted *and constrained* popular rights; it focused on duties rather than rights of imperial subjects, and made no concessions regarding the rights of women. Indeed, the liberation of women remained regarded as one of the principle moral dangers of political modernization in Japan – the women's rights movements of the West were seen as symptoms that Europe had become morally defunct. The constitution granted *and constrained* popular politics; it provided for a parliament with an elected lower house (with suffrage restricted to about 5% of the male population), and real power remained extra-parliamentary, in the hands of the *genrô* and increasingly in the hands of the military, who each enjoyed direct access to the emperor himself, who remained the locus of sovereignty. One of the greatest successes of the *genrô* strategy was that it forestalled any possible discussion of making Japan into a republic, and hence preserved the underlying infrastructure that would become known as the *tennô-sei* (emperor system).

Social and political reform of the Meiji state

All of these innovative ideas and modern legal reforms were only meaningful to the people of Japan if they had real effects on everyday life. In particular, they rested upon domestic social reform and the abolition of the so-called *shi-nô-kô-shô* system of stratification, which separated the population into four classes (samurai, farmer, artisan, merchant) and provided for very little social mobility. Ironically, then, the first task of the revolutionaries, who were largely samurai themselves, was to abolish the privileges of their own class. It is a testament to the new regime's commitment to modernization that they were willing and able to do this. Of course, not all the samurai in Japan were equally visionary about the demands of modernity, and a significant number attempted to preserve their traditional prerogatives. Hence, the revolutionary Meiji regime had to move firmly but carefully lest it provoke a counter-revolution.

The *genrô* clique moved quickly to capitalize on the momentum of the Restoration. Led by the dynamic figures of Kido Kôin and Saigo

Takamori, the status of the daimyo was radically transformed within three years, and the samurai class as a whole was abolished within seven. Kido, Saigo, and other revolutionary leaders such as Yamagata Aritomo led by example, surrendering their own lands to the emperor in 1869, and then receiving appointments from the emperor as salaried governors of the same lands. The result was that they kept their power and status, but the symbolism of their subordination to the imperial house was powerful, since it figured a *unified nation* as an essentially *imperial realm*.

After surrendering their own lands in 1869, the *genrô* and the emperor established a Council of the State in 1871; they unilaterally abolished all 280 traditional *han*, reorganizing them into 72 prefectures (which are the basis of today's regional units). Some of the new governors were not even of daimyo status, but rather were talented samurai or even *heimin* (commoners). However, the daimyo were generously compensated and most were content with the new arrangements, which provided for their continuing comfort but removed the burden of their responsibilities.

One important side-effect of this move was, for the first time in Japanese history, a national, imperial army could be unified under a single flag and drawn from the powerful, outlying domains of Satsuma and Chôshû.

The great pioneer of the modern Japanese army was Yamagata Aritomo, who would become Japan's first prime minister under the Meiji Constitution in 1889 (the third prime minister in Japanese history) and also a Field Marshal in the Imperial Army in 1898. Under his influence Emperor Meiji invited military experts from Europe and the USA to train his new troops in the use of modern firearms and munitions.

It was Yamagata who pushed through the establishment of a national army, which commenced as a force of 10,000 samurai, but which became a conscript army in 1873; universal conscription for three years for all men over 20 came into force in that year. In combination with all the other reforms of the 1870s, the creation of a conscript army was seen by various samurai factions in Japan as the last straw; it seemed to challenge the last privilege and duty of the samurai class – the right to carry a sword and to defend the realm. Even some of the *genrô* who had happily surrendered lands and titles to the emperor, found this a step too far. Indeed, 1873 was also the year in which Yamagata Aritomo and Kido Shôin were forced to cut short the Iwakura Mission in order to return to Japan and block the plans of fellow *genrô* Saigo Takamori, for a samurai invasion of Korea. Saigo argued that an invasion would strengthen Japan's army and restore the vitality of the samurai; he even volunteered to travel to Korea to provoke an excuse for war by letting the Koreans kill him. Following the defeat of Saigo's plan, the Hizen samurai Etô Shimpei resigned from his position as a councillor to the new regime and returned to his hometown of Saga, where he organized disillusioned samurai into an ill-fated rebellion.

Yamagata's conscription edict might therefore be seen as *both* an attempt to modernize the Japanese army *and* as a necessary step to constrain and control the restive samurai. Indeed, the first significant military victory of Yamagata's modern, conscript army came in 1877 when it comprehensively defeated Saigo Takamori's samurai force in the Satsuma Rebellion. It wasn't long before Japan's Imperial Army, under the leadership of Yamagata, had also defeated China (1895) and Russia (1905).

One of the immediate economic advantages of the nationalization of Japan was the creation of a genuinely national taxation system for the first time in Japanese history. This meant that the central government could raise funds for a range of public works projects. Under the guidance of modernizers like Okubo Toshimichi, this meant not only the ability to build a national army, but it also gave the government the means to build a national railway and to construct 'model factories' for entrepreneurs and the business community to imitate and develop. The first stretch of railway, from Tokyo to nearby Yokohama, was completed in 1872, and within 20 years nearly 2,500 kilometers of track had been laid. The train was (and remains) an icon of industrial modernity, and it had been a potent symbol in the minds of the Japanese since Commodore Perry amazed them with his miniature locomotive in 1854. The role of the Japanese government here raises interesting questions about the proper role of the state in 'late-developing', or 'catch-up', economies.

In other words, national taxation provided the fuel for the construction of a modern economic system. It also generated widespread social change: the railways began to bring the outlying regions of Japan into easier reach of the capital in a way in which the Tokugawa could not even have dreamed, but also the growth of factories led to greater urbanization and radically transformed the lives of millions of Japanese.

However, the abolition of the *han* also brought with it many problems, including the huge financial burden of paying the stipends of all the samurai who used to draw their income from the daimyo. In 1871, this burden amounted to approximately 50% of state revenues, which very quickly, and understandably, became the source of significant public dissatisfaction: the samurai accounted for only a tiny proportion of the population.

In the end, a rapid incremental approach was adopted to phase out the samurai. The process began as early as 1869, when the number of samurai ranks were reduced to two, higher and lower. After three years, during which time all of the non-samurai in Japan had been reclassified as commoners, or *heimin* (ending the restrictions on dress, residency, and occupation that had characterized the Tokugawa system), the lower rank of samurai was blended into the *heimin*. In practice, of course, the *heimin* remained an internally differentiated group for many years. Various minorities stand out in this regard: foreigners were treated inconsistently – those from the West were granted great privileges, while those from Asia, who often arrived in Japan as war immigrants, were subjected to considerable discrimination; the social minorities known previously as *eta* or *hinin* (the unclean or non-persons) were recategorized as *burakumin* (hamlet people), which served to rename the problem rather than to solve it; and the largest disadvantaged group was women, who were prevented from enjoying any of the new liberties of the modern regime – rather, they were expected to be 'good wives and wise mothers', or tireless labourers in the emerging textile plants. Of course, there also remained great differentials in terms of wealth, values, and ways of life between the rapidly growing urban areas and the more traditional rural communities.

7. Women working in the Mitsui silk-reeling factory, *c.*1905

Indeed, when compulsory primary education was enforced, in 1872, some parts of Japan rioted in protest against the requirement to send their children to school rather than to send them out to work. Nonetheless, by the turn of the century nearly 98% of children attended primary education and higher education was beginning to blossom, meaning that the government could reform its own recruitment practices to hire people based on their performance in examinations (rather than based on heredity).

In 1873, the government decided to tax all samurai stipends, and then, in 1874, the government proposed a solution to samurai complaints about taxation, and offered to exchange their stipends for government bonds: those samurai who accepted this offer received very favourable returns. However, those who refused the offer found themselves forced to convert their stipends in 1876 (at a much less favourable rate), in which year the Meiji government also withdrew the samurai's right to wear swords in public, restricting this right to the police and military (many of whom were *heimin*). At this point, all of the prerogatives of the samurai had been systematically and incrementally revoked: they no longer held a privileged status; they no longer enjoyed an annual stipend; they no longer held the right to wear a sword; and they were no longer even entitled to an exclusive mode of dress or way of wearing their hair. By the time of Saigo's 1877 'samurai rebellion', the samurai no longer existed.

Towards a new nationalism

It is interesting to reflect, however, that the abolition of the samurai as a social class in Japan did not coincide with discarding the ostensible ideals of this warrior elite. Indeed, it is one of the paradoxes of Japan's engagement with modernity that it would quickly reinvent the image of the honourable and loyal samurai as a national emblem. Rather than representing an oppressive, unproductive, and expensive privileged elite from the feudal past, the samurai became re-imagined as the paragons of Japan's *national* values. Even the rebellion of Saigo Takamori was quickly romanticized as an act of glorious self-sacrifice in the name of the emperor – a small force of samurai stood against the unstoppable tide of modernity in order to show the Japanese people what it should mean to be Japanese, lest machines, industry, and commercialism cause the people to forget themselves. Just as Saigo had been willing to sacrifice himself in Korea in order to 'save' Japan, so the legend tells that he sacrificed himself in Japan in order to save it from itself. The moral force of this popular story was to affirm the fundamental value of Japanese traditions even in the face of the onslaught of Westernization and modernization: no matter how much it might change, Japan must remain Japan.

Perhaps the most influential proponent of the Way of the Samurai, or *bushidô*, as the 'soul of Japan' was Nitobe Inazo. Ironically, Nitobe saw *bushidô* as the answer to a problem of modernity: he saw that the Great Powers of Europe all had complex and deep-rooted systems of religious belief and ideology, which gave their nations a coherent sense of identity and moral worth; he worried that Japan lacked such a sense of national identity. Nitobe was not a great historian, but when he looked back through Japanese history he saw *bushidô* as a common thread (despite the fact that the term '*bushidô*' itself is a rather modern invention) and he presented it to the world as Japan's equivalent of European 'chivalry'. Indeed, Nitobe's famous book, *Bushidô: The Soul of Japan* (1899), was written in English for Western readers, and was only translated into Japanese later. Nonetheless, by the early 20th century, the idea of *bushidô* as a Japanese ideology, rather than a set of ideals for the samurai class, was firmly entrenched in the training of the conscript army and in society more broadly.

In many ways, the question of 'national identity' was one of the most pressing issues as Japan neared the 20th century, and it was also one of the issues that could be debated by the people themselves in the newly active public sphere. Magazines devoted to discussion about the meaning of 'Japaneseness' in the modern world started to appear. Led by intellectuals such as Okakura Tenshin and spurred on by foreign visitors such as Ernest Fenellosa, who were eager to unearth 'oddities' about the Japanese for consumption in Europe and the USA, a veritable industry of national self-interrogation began. Later academics would refer to this as the beginning of the so-called *Nihonjinron* literature (essays on Japanese uniqueness), which continues to be produced in the present day. This sense of identity crisis is often considered to be a universal symptom of the growing pains of modernity.

The issue took on multiple dimensions. On the one hand, some of Japan's greatest modern novelists, such as Natsume Sôseki, took the encounter with modernity as a central theme in their work. Sôseki, who travelled to England at the turn of century, returned to Japan overwhelmed by how depressing the dark, polluted industrial cities of England had become. Many of his most famous novels lament the loss of traditional Japanese values as they are engulfed in this industrial modernity. Other authors, like Okakura Tenshin himself, sought to define a distinctly Japanese aesthetic that could be identified in contradistinction to the flashy commercialism of modernity; without being able to identify 'Japanese' values, how could they be preserved?

And on the other hand, the laypeople attempted to discover the parameters of the new Japan, implicitly probing its borders with their actions. A very famous example is the case of Uchimura Kanzô, an English teacher at the First Higher School in Tokyo. In January 1891, Uchimura refused to bow to a copy of the Imperial Rescript on Education that had been signed by the emperor himself. He argued that the Meiji Constitution guaranteed him freedom of conscience and that, as a Christian, it would be a violation of his faith to force him to bow to this idol.

Unfortunately, neither the authorities nor his colleges were sympathetic, and Uchimura was eventually forced to resign his post amidst a storm of protest about his alleged treachery. The Uchimura incident reveals vestiges of the same kinds of suspicions about Christianity that had led the Tokugawa regime to ban it, but it also reveals some of the core elements of Japan's evolving national identity. In particular, it shows that the person and symbol of the emperor himself was inviolable: freedoms and rights would be protected only to the extent that they did not infringe upon a subject's duty to the emperor.

In other words, the embrace of modernity in Meiji Japan had its particularities. Whilst Japan was transformed from a semi-feudal political federation with a loosely integrated economy and stunted foreign policy into a unified national polity with a national economy and an emerging international presence, its identity and unity was closely bound to the traditional symbol of the emperor. Of course, a number of modern European states also had monarchies, and eventually the West did recognize Japan's modernity by ending the Unequal Treaties at the end of the 19th century.

However, even while Japan was absorbing Western technology, medicine, literature, and philosophy, the Japanese were already attempting to define and preserve the distinctive features that made them 'Japanese'. One of these features was the emperor himself: Japan was an imperial polity. As we will see in the next chapter, this imperial identity, combined with the accumulation of significant material power as well as European ideas about social evolution and the natural expansion of capital, would lead Japan along a path towards the attempt to 'overcome modernity' through war against its neighbours and ultimately against the democracies of Europe and the USA.

Chapter 3
Overcoming and overcome by modernity: Japan at war

The tremendous changes that engulfed Japan during the second half of the 19th century were initially inspired by a sense of national humiliation and insecurity in the face of the so-called Great Powers of the Western world. However, as Japan successfully adopted the ideas and trappings of modernity and freed itself from the Unequal Treaties that had been imposed on it, national confidence soared. Whilst some sectors of Japanese society chose to embrace the idea that modernity was a full package, containing not only technological innovations but also social mores and cultural practices, other sectors began to use this newfound confidence as an opportunity to challenge the notion that modernization and Westernization necessarily meant the same thing. Now that Japan had entered the modern world, the most pressing question seemed to shift away from what it meant to be 'modern in modern Japan' and towards a more personal question of what it meant to be Japanese in the first place.

On the one hand, we might identify a romantic response to this question. Intellectuals, writers, artists, and activists looked to the imagined past of Japan for a sense of what the 'essence' of Japaneseness might be: for some, this meant a reinvention of *bushidô* as the 'soul of Japan', or Shintô as a national religion and emperor cult; for others, it might have meant the rediscovery of a particular appreciation of a fragile, shadowy beauty that characterized Japanese aesthetics. In other words, one of the core challenges of modernity was the way in which it forced Japanese society to be self-reflective about its own identity, provoking a new literature that has come to be called *Nihonjinron* (essays on Japanese uniqueness). For many, the question was how this identity could be reconciled with the demands of the modern world.

On the other hand, we might identify a more chauvinistic response. From this perspective, the core dilemma was not how to preserve elements of 'Japaneseness' amidst the radical changes that accompanied modernization, but rather how to confront the process of modernization itself. This position radicalized Japanese traditions (whether invented or not) and asserted their superiority over those of the Western nations, which thus risked polluting and weakening Japan under the false guise of progress. As the confidence and power of Japan grew, this chauvinism held the potential to slip into an aggressive sense of mission: Japan had a moral duty to reassert its own authentic identity, and this duty implied a moral mission to help other Asian nations to overcome the insidious infection of modernity and Westernization. In short, this position provided the conditions of possibility for a paradoxically anti-imperialist imperialism in Asia; Japan's mission was to free Asia from the grip of Western imperialism.

The politics of the Meiji empire

As discussed in the previous chapter, the Meiji Restoration and the revolution that followed it was essentially imperial in character. In the so-called Age of Empires, it seemed very natural to the political and military elites that their new imperial state should also have an empire of its own, like the Great Powers of the West whose empires had already spread their tendrils throughout Asia. It was with this kind of thinking in mind that Yamagata Aritomo, fresh from his trip to Europe, endeavoured to build a powerful Japanese navy, in imitation of the navy of the greatest imperial power of the day, the small island nation of Great Britain.

Although Saigo Takamori's plans for an invasion of Korea in the early 1870s were thwarted by the *genrô* (who cut short the Iwakura Embassy in Europe in order to prevent it), and by Yamagata Aritomo in particular, the government's objection to the plan was not its imperial ambition but rather the method and rationale of the venture. Indeed, in 1876 Yamagata himself argued that Korea was an essential part of Japan's 'zone of advantage' and that its relative weakness (as a less modern society) both made it vulnerable to Japan's regional ambitions and to the ambitions of the West, which in turn constituted a vulnerability for Japan itself. It was imperative, he argued, that Korea should fall into Japan's sphere, since it was certain to fall to someone.

With this kind of imperial competition in mind, and conscious of Japan's new power on the regional stage, Japan imposed the Treaty of Kanghwa on Korea in 1876. The process was almost a precise duplication of the way that Commodore Perry had imposed the Treaty of Kanagawa on Japan just twenty years earlier, and its terms were similarly exploitative. Until Korea modernized, Yamagata and others argued that it was not worthy of an equal treaty. Hence, throughout the 1880s Japan sent emissaries to Korea to advise it on how to modernize its education system, its economy, and its political structure, just as Japan was receiving similar advice from Europe.

The situation in Korea was very complicated, not least because of the traditional competition between Japan and China for influence over the peninsula. The Treaty of Kanghwa as well as the presence of so many Japanese advisors aggravated the Chinese rulers as well as many Korean people. In Japan, opinion leaders attempted to reconcile the apparent hypocrisy of Japanese foreign policy through recourse to the rhetoric of Pan-Asianism: Japan was helping Korea to help itself, as an Asian brother helps another under threat from the West. Nonetheless, violence against the Japanese emissaries in Korea was not infrequent, until finally in 1894 there was a full-scale uprising against foreign influence. The Tonghak Rebellion, which was partially a religious movement, partially popular xenophobia, and partially anti-Japanese in sentiment, undermined stability in Korea to such an extent that the leaders called for military aid from their traditional patrons, China, in order to restore order. Greatly offended by this, and under the pretext of defending their zone of advantage, the Japanese sent troops of their own into Korea, where they came into conflict with the Chinese. The result was the first Sino-Japanese War of modern times.

Thanks to the modernization drive instigated by Yamagata Aritomo, the Japanese army was vastly superior to that of its giant neighbour. In addition, in pursuit of a 'British Empire for

8. **Postcard showing Japan trampling Korea on the way to Russia**

Japan', Japan had built an impressive navy; for the first time in history it enjoyed naval parity with China, and technological superiority. The outcome of the war was a clear victory for Japan, whose privileged position in Korea was therefore confirmed. Moreover, as compensation for the war, Japan claimed the island of Taiwan (Formosa), the small but strategically important Liaodong peninsula on the Chinese mainland, and a huge cash indemnity from China.

The Sino-Japanese War was a great success and extremely popular with the people of Japan, who had been becoming very dissatisfied with the expense and privilege of the military. Various justifications for Japan's imperial project emerged from the public sphere, ranging from appeals to Social Darwinism and the survival of the fittest ('either empire or colony!'), through the natural process of the expansion of a modern, capitalist economy, to romantic appeals to a project of nation-building. In the case of the latter, the Japanese public were fed a series of ideological constructions over the next several decades, beginning perhaps with the so-called Mito ideology, which mixed ideas about Confucian piety and Shintô myths to produce a vision of Japan as the divine centre of a regional order, with a moral mission to bring the light of the emperor to the people of Asia.

Suffice it to say that the public increasingly felt a sense of ownership over political issues: Japan was *their* nation. Indeed, the drive for popular participation in politics had been strong since the first election under the new constitution in 1890, at which the two largest parties (Liberal and Progressive) won 171 of the 300 seats contested in the lower house. Despite the fact that suffrage was limited to 1% of the population (male and in the highest tax bracket), the parliamentarians as well as the electorate were serious about supporting social welfare measures and thus about exercising their power to set the national budget. Civil society more widely was alive with these debates, in the press, in rallies, and protest.

Meanwhile, the *genrô*, their pro-government party (which returned less than 80 seats in 1890), and the unelected house of peers were extremely sceptical about allowing the 'common people' such influence over national decisions, especially military budgets. In fact, while the political parties were critical of the high levels of military spending that Yamagata insisted were necessary for the defence of Japan's 'sphere of advantage', they were not terribly interested in reallocating budgets to improve the lot of the masses: the rights of factory workers were largely neglected until 1911, when a very weak Factory Act was passed; and women remained banned from political meetings until the 1920s. Indeed, euphoria over the Sino-Japanese War served to change popular orientation towards war budgets for the next decade (in 1895 the parliament even voted for a bill that would increase the tax on big business to increase the government's budget) and it lasted until about 1905, when there were riots in Hibiya Park in central Tokyo, protesting against the military, its expense, and its apparent failure, despite its victory in the Russo-Japanese War.

Not all the European Great Powers were as sanguine about Japan's victory against China as the British, who applauded their accomplishments and soon terminated their Unequal Treaties. As soon as the terms of the Treaty of Shimonoseki became public, a joint ultimatum was issued by the governments of Russia, France, and Germany, demanding that Japan retrocede the Liaodong peninsula. For Russia in particular, which had its own ideas about a sphere of influence in China, this small but strategic peninsula gave Japan an unacceptable advantage in the region. An embittered Japan, whose public saw this Triple Intervention as Western duplicity, had no choice but to withdraw its troops. The sense of resentment only grew when Russia itself occupied the peninsula shortly afterwards, and other European powers took advantage of a weakened China to seize other city-ports. To many in Japan, the Triple Intervention and the events that followed it looked like simple racism: although Japan had met all the criteria of a 'modern nation' and had liberated itself from the Unequal Treaties, it was still not taken seriously as an international actor.

In fact, the struggle with Russia was just beginning. The interest of all of the Great Powers in establishing spheres of interest in Asia, and particularly in China, brought them into direct military contact. At the turn of the century, Japan joined an international coalition that included the British and the Russians to combat the anti-foreign Boxer Uprising in northern China (1899–1901). Subsequently, Japan attempted to gain formal recognition of its claims in Korea from the British and the Russians. In 1902, Japan achieved a great diplomatic coup when it signed an alliance with the British Empire, according to the terms of which Britain would recognize Japan's claims in Korea and would cooperate with Japan against the expansion of Russian influence in the region. This was the first formal alliance that Great Britain had signed with a non-Western power, and it was met with great fanfare in Japan as an indication that the nation had come of age. However, no such recognition was forthcoming from Russia itself.

Buoyed by the Anglo-Japanese alliance, former prime minister Itô Hirobumi proposed the so-called *Mankan kôkan* (exchange of Manchuria for Korea), an agreement that offered Japanese acknowledgement of Russian preponderance in Manchuria in return for Russian acknowledgement of Japan's special interests in Korea. However, the proposal was rejected in Moscow. In Tokyo this rejection was interpreted as confirmation of Russia's hostile intent, and diplomatic relations were severed. Three hours before it issued a formal declaration of intent, the Japanese Empire attacked the Russian Far Eastern Fleet at Port Arthur, on the Liaodong peninsula. The Imperial Japanese Navy proceeded to effect some stunning defeats against the Russian Fleet, besieging and taking Port Arthur and then comprehensively defeating the famed Baltic Fleet in a single day in the Tsushima Straits (27–28 May 1905). The Baltic Fleet had literally sailed all the way around the world, via the Cape of Good Hope, to break the siege at Port Arthur (which had already fallen by the time it arrived), and the Japanese victory under the command of Admiral Tôgô astonished the world. Indignant that they could not have been defeated so easily by the Japanese, rumours in Moscow suggested that the Baltic Fleet had been destroyed by the British navy in disguise – rumours without any foundation. Admiral Tôgô Heihachirô, who had indeed trained in Great Britain in the 1870s, earned himself the epithet of the 'Nelson of the East' after the Battle of Tsushima. A lock of Nelson's hair was presented to him by the Royal Navy to commemorate his achievement, and Yamagata Aritomo received the Order of Merit from King Edward VII in 1906.

Japan's victory sent shockwaves around the international community; it was the first time that a European power had been defeated by an Asian power in the modern era. Russia's military capacity had been devastated, and its prestige severely dented – indeed, the humiliation of the defeat was one of the factors that provided the backdrop for the Russian Revolution of 1917. Yet, despite the drama, the heroics, and the victory, the Russo-Japanese War was not a great success for Japan. The terms of the Treaty of Portsmouth that ended the war reflected the fact that both sides had suffered terrible losses and gained little. Japan had succeeded in demonstrating its power – as equal or superior to that of one of the Great Powers – and hence it consolidated its regional position: Russia recognized its claims in Korea, which it would quietly annex in 1910. Furthermore, Russia was forced to hand over its 25-year lease on Port Arthur, returning it to Japan and thus reversing the Triple Intervention. And finally Japan acquired (only) the southern half of the island of Sakhalin. However, there was no massive cash indemnity, as there had been at the close of the Sino-Japanese War, and the Japanese public found this unacceptable – there were even riots in protest in some of Japan's major cities.

Support for the military and its spending diminished in the parliament and amongst the public at large. Indeed, for the next decade there were frequent protests and riots in the urban centres about military spending set against the cost of public transport and rice, as well as demonstrations in favour of expanded suffrage.

During the same period, unionization and 'friendly societies' started to gain in popularity, and support for a fledgling socialist movement began to appear. A Social Democratic Party was founded in 1901, but was instantly banned. The movement radicalized into anarchism and communism under the leadership of activists like Kôtoku Shusui and Katayama Sen, who would eventually be executed for High Treason in 1911. The orthodoxy of Japan's nation-building project, even in the wake of the Russo-Japanese War, never embraced the political left, since it threatened to challenge the one emblem that held the whole Meiji state together: the figure of the emperor himself.

Hence, the death of Emperor Meiji in 1912 was a real turning point in modern Japanese history. Meiji had overseen the unification of Japan into a single nation-state, and then the modernization of that state into one that could stand equally with those of the West as an imperial power. However, at the time of his death, Japan was already witnessing the start of a new phase of politics, as popular opinion turned against the militarization of the state and sought to forge Japan into a genuinely participatory democracy. Political parties became more coherent and more focused on issues, rather than simply clubs that parliamentarians joined. Indeed, in the year of Meiji's death, the leader of the Seiyûkai party, Hara Kei, succeeded in forcing a stalemate with the military about its new budget. Not even the elder statesman Yamagata Aritomo could resolve the situation in favour of the military, and this ushered in a period that has come to be known as the 'politics of compromise'. Hara would go on to become Japan's first commoner, party-based prime minister in 1918.

Taishô democracy

Emperor Taishô ruled for a brief period between 1912 and 1926, when the Shôwa emperor, who would reign until his death in 1989, succeeded him. For many historians, the Taishô period appears like a small window of calm in the middle of a century of war and struggle for Japan. Intellectuals and activists such as Yoshino Sakuzô advocated a kind of democracy called *minponshugi* (rule for the people), which he argued was compatible with Japan's constitutional monarchy. At the same time, constitutional lawyers such as Minobe Tatsukichi argued that the emperor might best be considered an 'organ' in the overall structure of the state, rather than as coterminous with the nation as a whole. Meanwhile, internationalists like Nitobe Inazo placed their faith in the emergence of a new world order that would recognize diversity and multicultural membership; Nitobe himself was an undersecretary-general of the League of Nations from 1920 and a founding director of the International Committee on Intellectual Cooperation (the forerunner of UNESCO).

Against this background, a new middle class was emerging in the rapidly growing urban centres. This was the birth of the so-called salaryman (*sarariman*) – the ubiquitous, white-collared worker. But this period also saw a new class of white-collared women working as 'office ladies' or as attendants in shops. In general, women in these jobs were very poorly paid, but they featured in popular culture as icons of modern life: flashy and fashionable, immersed in the consumerism of products and fads, and often represented as morally liberal, selling kisses as well as Western clothes to their customers. These were the *moga* or *modan gaaru* (modern girls). The new middle class (which contrasted with the 'old middle class' of former samurai families) was represented as liberal and free, moving regularly between different jobs at different companies and enjoying the trappings of modern life.

This new way of life cohabited with a new culture, and the Taishô period saw the Japanese enthusiastically embrace many American pastimes: baseball and jazz being the most pervasive. But there were also developments in Japan's own artistic ferment, with arguably modern Japan's greatest authors, such as Akutagawa Ryûnosuke and Tanizaki Juni'ichirô, writing darkly beautiful short stories and novels that contemplated questions of individual and cultural identity in Japan's rapidly changing society. At the same time, there was a flourishing of avant-garde poetry and art. The advent of the 'one yen' book, the further development of national and local newspapers, and the establishment of rental stores for novels, magazines, and manga (graphic fiction) brought these materials to an ever wider and increasingly educated public.

Of course, this middle class image of Taishô Japan was not the whole story. The working class factory workers that so characterized the Meiji period found their conditions largely unchanged. Again, it was young women who bore the brunt of this, with men toiling under similarly harsh conditions in heavier industry. However, the Taishô period also saw the working classes becoming increasingly conscious of their plight and their power: workers began to organize into unions and 'friendly societies', even the *burakumin* began to participate in social activism in the form of the *Suiheisha* (Levellers' Association). Local disputes and strikes increased in number throughout the 1920s, as activists started to embrace liberal and even communist ideas.

The image of the Taishô period as a war-free haven is at least partially premised upon the economic boom that Japan experienced during the years of the Great War in Europe. During the war years, Japanese industrial output increased by a factor of five as it sought to supply European and domestic demand, and its exports surged (especially textiles).

9. Modernity at the crossroads, *c.*1928

For the first time in modern history, Japan became a net creditor nation.

Historians often overlook Japan's role in World War I: it joined the war at the request of its ally, Great Britain, on 23 August of 1914, and then quickly occupied the German territories in East Asia, including Shangdong and Tsingtao. The Imperial Navy proceeded to occupy a string of Germany's island colonies in October, including the Marshall Islands. Furthermore, Japan used the instability in the region to consolidate its position in Manchuria and to assert itself against a weakened China – issuing the so-called Twenty-One Demands for economic and territorial concessions. Elsewhere, Japan was involved in a joint campaign with the USA to attempt to bolster the 'Whites' in the Russian Revolution, which erupted in 1917, and it also sent a naval squadron of 17 ships to the Mediterranean to help escort British vessels based at Malta. Indeed, Japan's involvement in World War I earned it a seat amongst the Big Four (Britain, France, USA, and Italy) in Versailles for the negotiation of the peace treaty in 1919, and also a permanent seat on the Council of the League of Nations – an achievement that postwar Japan has not accomplished in the United Nations.

This recognition by the Western powers was met with enthusiasm back in Japan. However, the Japanese delegation at the conference did not get everything that it wanted. Although they successfully lobbied to keep their territorial acquisitions in Asia, their second goal – the inclusion of a racial equality clause in the Preamble to the Covenant of the League of Nations – was thwarted. Former prime minister and *genrô* Saionji Kinmochi led the Japanese delegation, which proposed the following clause to the conference:

> The equality of nations being a basic principle of the League of Nations, the High Contracting Parties agree to accord as soon as possible to all alien nationals of states, members of the League, equal and just treatment in every respect making no distinction, either in law or in fact, on account of their race or nationality.

In fact, a majority of the seventeen delegations present voted to support this clause, including all of the non-European representatives (except the USA). In principle this meant that the motion could be carried. However, US President Woodrow

74

Wilson, who was chairing the session, overthrew the decision, stating that although a majority carried the motion, opposition to it was so serious that it should require unanimity for this proposal to pass. In practice, Wilson was talking about opposition from the British, for whom such a measure would spell the end of its empire, and Wilson realized that the emergent League of Nations needed British support more than it needed Japanese support (especially after the USA itself failed to join).

This failure at Versailles was not well received back in Japan, where protests erupted in the streets. For many commentators at the time (and since), this looked like another example of Western racism, echoing the duplicity that the Japanese perceived at the time of the Triple Intervention. The feeling of injustice was severe, especially since Japan at the turn of the 1920s had become a modern, constitutional democracy with an imposing empire and a flourishing economy: it had met all of the objective criteria to join the club of modern nations, but it was still being refused entry. It seemed, finally, that being modern was not enough: modern Japan would never be considered an equal partner in international affairs for as long as it was Japanese. This was the one thing that Japan could do nothing about, and indeed it was becoming increasingly assertive about the importance of maintaining its distinctive identity. Events at Versailles added fuel to the fires of Japanese romantics and chauvinists who were striving to rediscover, reinvent, or simply protect 'Japaneseness' in the modern state.

Only two years later, Britain allowed the Anglo-Japanese alliance to lapse and instead proposed a five-way naval agreement involving the USA, France, and Italy. The so-called Washington Naval Treaty of 1921, one of a number of such treaties to be signed over the next decade or so, obliged the signatories to maintain a fixed ratio of naval power (measured in tonnage of capital ships and aircraft carriers). As far as Japan was concerned, the key ratio was Britain:USA:Japan, which was set at 5:5:3, meaning that Japan would always be less powerful than the two nations that thwarted its racial equality clause. But, perhaps the last straw for those in Japan who saw a systematic racism at work in the Anglo-American world was the enactment of the 1924 immigration laws in the USA, which specifically prohibited the immigration of East Asians.

Unfortunately, this perception of an unsympathetic international environment coincided with economic collapse in Japan, which followed the wartime bubble, and natural catastrophe in the form of the great Kanto earthquake of 1923, which left 150,000 people dead or missing and about half a million residences in Tokyo levelled. By the end of the Taishô period, Japan was in depression, the *zaibatsu* conglomerates (such as Mitsubishi, Mitsui, and Sumitomo) were beginning to take over the economy as private banks failed, and they were cultivating ever-closer connections with the political parties and the military. This meant that wealth was being concentrated into fewer hands, and more of the urban population was struggling to maintain their way of life. Hence, by the start of the increasingly militaristic Shôwa period, Japan was ripe for change once again: the democratic window appeared to be closing.

Early Shôwa and war in the Pacific

Following the collapse of the New York Stock Market in 1929, economic depression swept the globe. Japan took the yen off the gold standard in 1931 and watched its value slump by 50% against the dollar. Unemployment rose dramatically, quickly reaching over 20%. In the urban centres, where the modern life of Taishô had seemed so exciting, the darker underside of the modern condition became readily apparent. Intellectuals started to write about the crisis of capitalism and the angst of modern life. Despite being illegal after the 1925 Peace Preservation Law, the communist movement simmered in the universities. The emblems of urban chic – the *moga* waitresses and shop attendants – gradually became seen as euphemisms for prostitutes in the popular imagination. Modernity began to look like an infection that threatened the soul and even the wellbeing of Japan, rather than a material boon. The people of Japan, already struggling in the late 1920s, turned their frustrations against the political parties, accusing them of being the 'running dogs of capitalism'. Clandestine political movements began to agitate.

The early 1930s saw political violence rise to an all-time high, and a number of commentators have referred to it as the period of 'government by assassination'. The first victim was Prime Minister Hamaguchi Osachi, who was shot in Tokyo Station by a member of an ultranationalist group in 1930, following his failure to secure a more equal naval treaty with the British and Americans at the London Naval Conference earlier that year. In the following year, government authorities discovered and thwarted two separate plots for a *coup d'état*. In 1932, the next prime minister, Inukai Tsuyoshi, was assassinated by a clandestine group of naval officers after he failed to support actions by the Imperial Kwantung Army in Manchuria. This series of events at the start of the 1930s effectively ended parliamentary rule and marked the move towards greater military control of governance. Whilst large sections of the population reacted with horror to these developments, the military could count on significant support particularly in rural areas. The promise of imperial greatness, of a return to the glories of Meiji, provided an enticing distraction from the problems of the time.

Meanwhile, the military itself had also grown factional and restive. In particular, the Kwantung Army, which had been created in 1906 to protect Japan's interests in Manchuria, began to agitate for action. The commander in the field, Colonel Ishiwara Kanji, had a millenarian vision of the coming of the 'final war' in which the nations of the world would be punished for the moral corruptions of modernity. His solution was to propose that Japan should take over Manchuria and use it as a social laboratory to test new and better forms of organization; he wanted to forge a new post-capitalist society based on non-selfish principles. His motivation was largely Buddhist rather than Communist. To this end, without orders from Tokyo, the Kwantung Army orchestrated an attack on the Manchurian railway, which they were supposed to be guarding. They exploded a section near Mukden and proceeded to blame the attack on local Chinese forces, using this as a pretext to launch an offensive and the formal occupation of Manchuria. In Tokyo, this *fait accompli* was greeted with shock by then Prime Minister Inukai, who refused to condone the annexation of Manchuria as a colony. After his assassination, the puppet state of Manchukuo was formed in March 1932. This 'Manchuria Incident' marked the start of the so-called Fifteen Years' War between China and Japan. In the depressed environment of Japan at the time, a majority of the Japanese people received news of the Kwantung Army's victories and the expansion of the empire with jubilation.

The international community, in the form of the League of Nations, in which Japan had played a leading role, took measures to condemn the occupation. It refused to recognize Manchukuo as an independent state, and its Lytton Report called for Japan to withdraw its forces from Manchuria in February 1933. But this was too little too late. In Japan, the condemnation of the League merely confirmed the duplicity of the Western powers, and particularly the British who dominated the council. Japan simply withdrew from the League, claiming that it would now 'follow its own path in Asia', implicitly accusing the League of being a regional rather than a universal organization (a charge that was not without justification). A result was that many Japanese felt vindicated in their beliefs that the Western powers were fundamentally racist against Japan and Asia more widely; Japan became increasingly isolated from the international community and hence increasingly reliant on its own military power.

Japan's 'own path in Asia' unravelled quickly in Japan. Within five years, the military had appropriated nearly 75% of the national budget, and much of the decision-making about foreign policy and domestic budgets was being made in discussion between factions of the military, the leaders of which enjoyed direct access to the emperor under the principle of the independence of supreme command, enshrined in the Meiji Constitution. Inspired by the radical work of Kita Ikki, unsatisfied with the ongoing vestiges of party politics, and arguing that Japan had lost the authentically imperial spirit of the Meiji Restoration, a group of officers from the so-called Imperial Way Faction (*kôdô-ha*) launched a military *coup d'état*. On 26 February 1936, the group seized control of downtown Tokyo, executing the finance minister and former prime minister Saitô, but mistakenly assassinating Prime Minister Okada's brother-in-law instead of Okada himself. The group then called on Emperor Shôwa to announce a Shôwa Restoration, which would place him in direct control of the Imperial Army and launch a new era of imperial glory for Japan.

The emperor was apparently horrified by this egregious breach of the constitutional order, and the coup was finally quashed by troops from the competing Control Faction (*tôsei-ha*), which included future prime minister and general Tôjô Hideki. Rather than breaking the control of the military, however, this coup served to consolidate the power of the Control Faction.

In an attempt to constrain the military, the last surviving *genrô*, Saionji Kinmochi, recommended Prince Konoe Fumimaro as the next prime minister. However, even the eminent Konoe could not constrain the army's ambitions. Within a few weeks of his taking office, on 7 July 1937 the Imperial Army exchanged fire with Chinese soldiers at the Marco Polo Bridge, south of Beijing. It is not clear who fired first, but many historians argue that the Japanese Army manufactured this skirmish as a pretext for escalation. Whatever the truth of this, it is certainly true that the Imperial Army was ambitious for further action in China.

In the end, Konoe himself was an advocate of Japanese expansionism. Rather than trying to restrain the army in China, he authorized the escalation of the conflict, and the army immediately launched a massive offensive. By mid-December, Japanese forces had pushed south from Beijing as far as Shanghai and Nanjing. The conduct of the Imperial Army in Nanjing was horrifying and mystifying. Japanese troops herded together tens of thousands of civilians and surrendered soldiers and murdered them; they raped and killed perhaps 20,000 women of all ages. The total number of casualties is still contested to this day, with numbers ranging from tens of thousands to 300,000 deaths. The terrible violence continued for nearly two months. The question of why the Imperial Army behaved in this appalling way, and why the High Command permitted the atrocities to continue for nearly two months has still not received a satisfactory answer.

A small number of right-wing revisionists in contemporary Japan argue that the Nanjing Massacre never happened; they claim that it was invented by the victorious Allied Powers after the end of the war as a means to further punish and victimize the Japanese. A famous example of this view can be found in the controversial manga of Kobayashi Yoshinori, *Sensôron* (On War, 1998). Some high school history textbooks in Japan refer to the events in neutral terms as the Nanjing Incident (*Nankin jiken*) rather than as the Nanjing Massacre (*Ninkin daigyakusatsu*), triggering protests of atrocity-denial in China. This 'textbook controversy', which also involves the under-representation of so-called 'comfort women' (sexual slaves of the Imperial Army) still rages to this day. Historians such as Inega Saburô filed lawsuits against the Ministry of Education for trying to censor their frank disclosure of Japanese wartime atrocities. Ienaga's fight was highly publicized around the world: Noam Chomsky nominated him for the Nobel Peace Prize (1999, 2002).

After the initial push south, the war in China gradually ground to a stalemate in late 1938. Spurred on by the Anti-Comintern Pact, which Japan had co-signed with Nazi Germany in 1936 (and Italy in 1937), the Japanese army decided to push north into Siberia instead. However, the epic tank battle at Nomohan in the summer of 1939 was so disastrous (for both the Japanese and the Soviet Union) that all plans for a northerly advance were abandoned, and a Neutrality Treaty was signed with the USSR in 1941 (following Hitler's Non-Aggression Treaty in the autumn of 1939).

With stability in the north and stagnancy in China, the Imperial Forces started to consider other options. After signing the Tripartite Pact with Germany and Italy in 1940, which was really targeted against the USA, Japan was able to move south into Indo-China, since the French Vichy regime were obliged to collaborate with Germany's allies. At this point, President Roosevelt, in an America struggling to maintain its policy of isolationism, drew a line in the sand and imposed an oil embargo on Japan unless it retreated from China. At the same time, after consolidating all of the political parties into a single *Taisei yokusankai* (Imperial Rule Assistance Association) and all the labour unions into the *Sanpô* (Patriotic Industrial Service Federation), Konoe was replaced by General Tôjô Hideki, who became the first prime minister of Japan to simultaneously hold offices as a full general and as Army Minister.

Tôjô's response to the American embargo was to see it as a noose around the neck of Japan, and he resolved to take dramatic action to break free of it. Rather than capitulate to pressure from the Anglo-American powers once again, Tôjô decided to launch a new offensive into Southeast Asia, against the British and Dutch territories, and also to make a definitive strike against the

10. The Pearl Harbor attack, 7 December 1941. *USS Maryland* can be seen alongside the capsized *USS Oklahoma*, while *USS West Virginia* burns

American Pacific Fleet in Pearl Harbor. On 7 December 1941 (8 December in Japan), the Japanese navy launched an all out attack against the USA, destroying two battleships, two destroyers, nearly 200 aircraft, and damaging at least ten other warships. The attack killed or wounded nearly 4,000 Americans. By contrast, the Japanese lost less than 30 aircraft and 65 men.

Like Japan's attack on Port Arthur in 1904, the strike against Pearl Harbor happened before a declaration of war was communicated. In fact, the declaration was delayed until just after the attack by the Japanese Embassy in Washington, where the staff took too long to decode and translate the message. Nonetheless, the fact of this 'surprise attack' (and the propaganda that was produced about it afterwards) played a significant role in mobilizing public opinion in the USA against Japan, and thus steeled the American people for the Pacific War that followed. By contrast, Tôjô and the planners in Tokyo had planned Pearl Harbor to be so devastating that the American public would lose all stomach for war with Japan and hence surrender quickly. The popular view of 'Americanism' in Japan at that time was of an uncultured land of bubblegum, tall buildings, and moral vacuity: it was modernity gone mad. This was perhaps Tôjô's biggest miscalculation.

Nonetheless, Pearl Harbor itself was counted a great victory against the USA. Singapore and the Malay Peninsula quickly fell from the British. The Philippines were taken, and the Dutch East Indies also fell to the Imperial Army. By 1942, the Japanese empire reached from Sakhalin in the north and swept down through Manchukuo, swathes of China, Korea, and Taiwan, and then back through the archipelagos of Southeast Asia to Japan. In Tokyo, a Great East Asia Ministry was established to administer the empire as a so-called 'co-prosperity sphere' (*kyôeiken*) – this was supposed to be the substance of Japan's 'own way in Asia'.

The ideology of an anti-imperial empire

In November of 1943, the leaders of the subjugated nations (or 'member states') were invited to Tokyo to participate in the first and only Greater East Asia Conference, at which the delegates were invited to discuss how best to organize the co-prosperity sphere for the mutual benefit of all the members. Pan-Asianism, which had been bubbling through Japanese public opinion since the Meiji period, became the rhetoric of the Japanese empire. In reality, Tokyo was finding it increasingly difficult to sustain its expansive empire, and it realized (too late) that it needed to cultivate the good will of its colonies. It also realized (again too late) that some of the other peoples of Asia were also fed up with Western imperialism, and that they might voluntarily join a movement that genuinely sought to throw the West out of Asia: Asia for the Asians. By this time, however, any pretence that Japan's empire was in any way anti-imperialist was horribly and offensively ridiculous.

Within Japan itself, the rhetoric of the co-prosperity sphere was hotly debated. In 1933, Konoe had established a 'brain trust', the *Shôwa kenkyûkai*, which was charged with drawing up plans for a New Order in East Asia. The members included the Kyoto School philosopher Miki Kiyoshi, whose essay '*Shin Nihon no shisô genri*' ('The Intellectual Principles of the New Japan', 1939) helped to establish the parameters of a vision of Japan and East Asia that had passed through modernity and challenged the imperialism of the West. In an attempt to 'clarify the national polity' with regard to these questions, the Ministry of Education published the notorious *Kokutai no hongi* (Fundamental Principles of our National Polity) in 1937. Between 1941 and 1942, four other members of the Kyoto School, including Nishitani Keiji, Kosaka Masaaki, Suzuki Shigetaka, and Koyama Iwao, held a series of public symposia themed on 'The World-Historical Standpoint and Japan', 'The Ethics and Historicity of the East Asian Co-Prosperity Sphere', and finally 'The Philosophy of All-Out War'. Intellectuals from other schools of thought also joined in the discussion in the famous 'Overcoming Modernity' symposium of July 1942. Even the father of modern Japanese philosophy, Nishida Kitarô, joined the debate when he wrote a short essay (apparently designed to be read by Tôjô himself) entitled 'Principles for a New World Order'.

The issues at stake in these debates were serious: how could Japan overcome the cultural hegemony of modernity *qua* Westernization and somehow pass through this borrowed modernity into an authentic modernity of its own; how could (and should) Japan help other nations in Asia to do the same thing; and finally how could Japan build a regional order that encompassed other nations in Asia without that order being an empire? The resolutions to these issues reached by the various voices remain contested to this day, and the debate about how/whether to overcome modernity itself has resurfaced in the postwar period in terms of Japan's desire to retain its identity in an increasingly Americanized world.

In fact, by the time that it organized the Great East Asia Conference, Japan was already losing the war. After defeat at the Battle of Midway in June 1942, at which Japan lost vital aircraft carriers, the tide had turned against it. By July 1944, when US forces captured Saipan, Japan was finally in range of Allied bombers and the war was basically lost. Tôjô resigned from office in the same month, and in February 1945 Prince Konoe petitioned the emperor to surrender in order to alleviate the terrible suffering of his people: the conditions of 'total war' had reduced much of Japan to extreme poverty and even starvation; air-raids and fire-bombings made the major cities almost uninhabitable. It is not clear whether Hirohito himself refused this petition, or whether it was refused for him by senior military officers who still believed in the possibility of a *tennôzan* (a divine victory). Whichever the case, the Japanese continued to fight with increasing ferocity and desperation: the so-called *kamikaze* (divine wind) suicide squadrons (officially these were 'special attack units' or *okubetsu kôgeki tai*) bombarded Allied shipping; during the terrible Battle of Okinawa, thousands of Japanese civilians fought the American invaders with sticks, rocks and bare fists, retreating back into the mountains until there was nowhere left to go, and then killed themselves to prevent capture. When Okinawa finally fell, a quarter of a million Japanese had died, including 150,000 civilians.

It is in the context of this kind of fanaticism that historians attempt to judge the necessity of the atomic bombings of Hiroshima and Nagasaki. Indeed, the dedication of the Japanese civilians and military led the US government to commission an anthropologist to attempt to explain why they were so devoted and what it might take to achieve final victory. The result, Ruth Benedict's famous monograph, *The Chrysanthemum and the Sword* (which was published in the form of a book in 1946), represents the start of Modern Japan Studies and its relationship with the US government in particular.

After threatening Japan's 'prompt and utter destruction' in the Potsdam Declaration of 26 July, the USA bombed Hiroshima on 6 August 1945, the USSR invaded Japan's Northern Territories on 8 August, and then the USA bombed Nagasaki on 9 August. Japan's situation was hopeless. But even then the chiefs of staff and the army minister refused to surrender unless the Allies would guarantee the survival of the emperor. The USA would only reply that they would leave the future of Japan in the hands of the Japanese people themselves, which did not reassure the Japanese elites who had always been so suspicious of the masses. Finally, Emperor Hirohito himself intervened on 14 August to break the deadlocked council, and he surrendered, making a radio broadcast to his shattered nation the next day. On 2 September, on board the *USS Missouri* in Tokyo Bay, the document of surrender was signed.

Given the terrible damage and suffering inflicted by them, the use of the atomic bombs against two Japanese cities, especially the second, are still the focus of controversy today. A particular question has been whether they were actually necessary, or whether Japan had already lost the war. It had no resources and no allies, its navy had been destroyed, it was vulnerable to air attacks on its cities, against her were assembled the powers of the USA, Britain, the USSR, and an emerging China. Could their use have been avoided? Various theories have been suggested, including that the USA dropped the bombs as part of a scientific experiment to see what effect they would have on a populated urban area, or that the bombs were designed primarily to intimidate the USSR, with a eye on the postwar settlement and the Cold War. However, when asked about the decision to drop the bombs, US Secretary of War Henry Stimson answered simply: '*it is seldom sound for the stronger combatant to moderate his blows whenever his opponent shows signs of weakening*'.

11. The mushroom cloud over Hiroshima reached more than 20,000 feet into the air

In his famous radio speech to the people of Japan, Emperor Hirohito singled out the A-bombs as part of the reason for his decision to surrender. He emphasized the moral and spiritual strength of the Japanese nation (and of the East Asian peoples), but stated bluntly that superior modern technology had tilted the balance in the war: Japan was overcome by modernity after all. Hirohito's words warned that the use of this kind of technology risked bringing about the end of civilization itself. His meaning is contested, but the spirit of his speech suggests that the Japanese should not allow the power of material technology to destroy their spirit or to eradicate their 'Japaneseness'; if modern technology is allowed to rule over everything, what is to become of the spirit that makes us human?

Postwar Japan should retain its spiritual wealth even in the face of saturation by modern technology.

Chapter 4

Economic miracles and the making of a postmodern society

A new start: the US occupation

In his first ever radio broadcast to the people of Japan, on 15 August 1945, Emperor Hirohito called on them to 'endure the unendurable and bear the unbearable'. The invincible and sacred Empire of Japan had been defeated; despite all the sacrifices, toil, and suffering, Japan had finally lost. In a surprisingly high-pitched voice, using archaic Japanese that many could not understand, the emperor apologized for the fact that the 'war had developed in a manner not necessarily to Japan's advantage'. He expressed his regrets to the Japanese themselves, but also (still clinging to the rhetoric of the co-prosperity sphere) to Japan's allies in East Asia. In an intriguing twist that would occupy historians and commentators for decades thereafter, Hirohito called on Japan to *endure* the changes that would inevitably follow, so that Japan could 'keep pace with the progress of the world', as though the impending reforms were instrumental measures to guarantee the survival of the 'innate glory of the imperial state'. In much the same way that Meiji revolutionaries had called for *wakon yôsai* (Japanese spirit and Western technology) as a strategy to both modernize Japan and to preserve its essence, so Hirohito seemed to suggest that a version of this strategy should be employed in the postwar period as well.

Reactions to the news of the defeat were diverse. On the one hand, there was an understandable incomprehension and despair: after all that the homeland population had been through, and after all that they had been told about the glories of the Imperial Army, how could the eternal empire have lost to the decadent and morally defunct West? For some, despair slid into dishonour, and approximately 350 military officers committed suicide to atone for their failure to protect the homeland. There was a sense of fear and apprehension, since the people had been told that the Americans were little more than monsters who would plunder the land and rape the women. For those in positions of power and influence, fear was more particular, and the night of 15 August was lit by the flames of great bonfires as records and incriminating documents were burned. But for many Japanese, the end of hostilities and the prospect of the arrival of the Americans brought a sense of relief and even hope: the war had been a terrible ordeal, and perhaps it was time for a change.

The reality of the occupation managed to meet the expectations of everyone. There was a level of humiliation for the Japanese. In fact, one of the first moves by the Japanese government was to organize 'comfort stations' (that is, brothels) to service American GIs. The American occupiers were quick to take advantage of this generous provision, although they finally banned state-sponsored stations in January 1946 as a violation of women's human rights (prostitution remained legal). There was a level of starvation and suffering, as the Japanese simply ran out of food and supplies, and the domestic economy slumped into collapse as though the tension had just been let out of it. The contrast with the well-fed Americans was stark, and a gloomy atmosphere of depression set into some of the major urban centres. But at the same time, the occupation brought opportunities for entrepreneurs – not just for pimps and prostitutes, but for translators and for businessmen of all kinds. And finally, it became immediately apparent that the Supreme Commander of Allied Powers (SCAP), US General Douglas MacArthur, had grand plans for the reconstruction of Japan; there would be new opportunities for everyone.

Although the occupation of Japan was technically a multilateral enterprise under the supervision of the Far Eastern Advisory Commission (which included representation from Australia, Britain, Canada, China, France, India, the Philippines, and the Netherlands), in practice it was an American show from the start. The USSR pushed for some involvement in the Allied Council on Japan, but MacArthur had already made substantial reforms in Japan before that body had its first meeting in February 1946. Washington was adamant that the new Japan would remain within its sphere of influence in the postwar international order.

Despite MacArthur's significant freedom to manoeuvre, he chose a tactic of indirect rule in order to maximize his effectiveness. In particular, realizing the symbolic value of the office, he decided immediately that the emperor should be protected and preserved. Indeed, sharing an insight that had been a commonplace throughout Japanese history, he feared that the abolition of the emperor might make the Japanese people ungovernable. Furthermore, for purely practical and linguistic reasons, MacArthur had to rely on a staff of Japanese interpreters and translators in order to get work done. Hence, SCAP employed a corps of bilingual political technicians to intervene between its government headquarters (GHQ) and the Japanese government itself, which was also retained. The result was that the Japanese authorities maintained the feeling (and to some degree the reality) of continuity and of being involved in the decision-making process, which helped MacArthur to push through his reforms, but which also left segments of the wartime and pre-war Japanese bureaucracy in place.

MacArthur's plans for reform were ambitious. Based on the assumption that wartime Japan had suffered from over-centralization, militarism, and fascism, he set out his plans

12. Hirohito and MacArthur, in 1945

according to two interlinked 'solutions to the Japan problem':
demilitarization and democratization.

The simplest of these was the first: MacArthur immediately
dissolved all of Japan's military forces, both within Japan and
beyond, which meant repatriating nearly 7 million people. He
disbanded the Special Higher Police (the so-called 'thought

police') that had monitored political criminals and intellectual dissidents during the war, and then he started his own purge of the politically offensive (removing 200,000 people from their posts in government, the bureaucracy, and business). Seeking to address the problem of the emperor cult, even if not the issue of the person of the emperor himself, SCAP then disestablished the state Shintô religion and forced the emperor to publicly renounce his divinity.

The showcase of the demilitarization campaign came in the form of the International Military Tribunal for the Far East (aka the Tokyo Trials), which were held between May 1946 and November 1948. These trials, which were designed to be the equivalent of the Nuremberg Trials in Germany, have been the subject of great controversy, and accusations of 'victor's justice' have been common; it is certainly the case that many more prisoners were executed in Tokyo than in Nuremberg, and some senior officers were executed for the unprecedented crime of 'conspiracy to wage war' rather than for war crimes themselves. The headline case was that of Tôjô Hideki himself, who was found guilty of war crimes and conspiracy to wage war, and was hanged. However, perhaps the most conspicuous aspect of these trials was the fact that MacArthur kept the emperor off the stand. For a number of postwar Japanese intellectuals, such as the political theorist Maruyama Masao, the failure to make the emperor face up to his responsibility was detrimental to MacArthur's second great ambition, the democratization of Japan, since it set a dangerous precedent that undermined the notion of political subjectivity that is essential for democratic consciousness.

Perceiving an apparent connection between militarism and monopoly economics, MacArthur's push for democracy began with measures to decentralize the economy. He affected a series of land reforms that forced landowners to sell all but a single plot of their holdings, thus enabling workers to own the land that they farmed. But the showpiece of economic democratization

13. The Tokyo Trials for war crimes

was the plan to dissolve the *zaibatsu* conglomerates, which
MacArthur associated with Japanese imperialism. SCAP was
convinced that these conglomerates had orchestrated the war
economies of Japan's colonies. In the end, however, the dissolution
of the *zaibatsu* was incompletely implemented. In many cases,
the family holding companies were dissolved, but the networks
quickly reformed around the banks that replaced them. The
resulting units, which shared some characteristics with the
zaibatsu, came to be known as *keiretsu*. The most famous names
in Japanese business – Mitsubishi, Mitsui, Fuji, Sumitomo,
Nissan – all continued into the postwar period.

In terms of social and political measures to promote democracy, SCAP immediately declared that it would protect the natural rights and freedoms of the Japanese citizens. For the first time in Japan's history, it announced the equal rights of women and minority groups. It gave workers the right to form unions and the right to strike. To promote intellectual freedoms, SCAP introduced education reforms (particularly to replace 'ethics' classes in which the *Kokutai no hongi* had been taught during the war), increased the compulsory level of education (to grade nine), and purged politically suspect professors. Furthermore, it outlawed (Japanese) censorship, although it engaged in censorship itself, and it declared an amnesty for political prisoners, which effectively meant releasing communist sympathizers.

In the political sphere, SCAP encouraged the development of new political parties, even though in practice these became re-fashionings of the wartime parties. Again, continuity was smuggled into reform. The *Seiyūkai* reformed as the *Jiyūtô* (the forerunner of today's Liberal Democratic Party, LDP), while the *Minseitô* reformed as the *Shinpotô* (Progressive Party). After a series of intrigues (and some covert support by the CIA), Yoshida Shigeru emerged as the first postwar prime minister, as leader of the Liberal Party in 1946. Indeed, the pro-American Yoshida would be prime minister on and off for the next eight years.

However, the showpiece of the democratization campaign was the promulgation of an entirely new constitution in November 1946 (coming into effect in May 1947). At first, MacArthur thought that it was important that the Japanese themselves took a leading role in the authorship of the document. In October 1945, he charged legal scholar Matsumoto Joji with forming a committee to redesign the constitution before December of that year (that is, before the first meeting of the Allied Council on Japan, in which sat the USSR). The so-called Matsumoto Committee made a series of recommendations for the new Japan, including strengthening the rights (and duties) of the Japanese people. However, Matsumoto's report recommended that the emperor should retain sovereignty (although the emperor should be encouraged not to exercise his power very often), and that elected officials and ministers should offer advice to the emperor. MacArthur found the Matsumoto report wholly unacceptable, and immediately commissioned the American chief of the Government Section, Courtney Witney, to draft something more suitable. In the end, partly due to a misunderstanding about the status of his document (which the Japanese authorities believed was being presented to them as the final text), it was Witney's draft that passed into law in 1947, almost unaltered by the Japanese themselves.

The 1947 constitution, which was technically promulgated by the emperor as an amendment of the Meiji constitution, transforms the emperor into 'the symbol of the unity of the Japanese people' and locates sovereignty in the people themselves. It guarantees the rights of the people on the model of the US Declaration of Rights, and it establishes a bicameral parliament on the Westminster model. Controversially, in Article 9, it also forbids Japan from developing an army, a navy, or any other 'war potential'. After more than 60 years, the 1947 constitution holds the singular distinction of being the oldest, unamended constitution in the world today.

However, the agenda of the occupation forces changed abruptly towards the end of 1947. The international environment was shifting after the Iron Curtain had fallen in Europe and the nationalist forces had started to stumble in China. The ideological and territorial ambitions of the Soviet Union were becoming clear in Washington, and this made MacArthur sensitive to the increasingly active labour movement and the growth of the political left in Japan. SCAP itself had released many leading communists from jail during the postwar amnesty, and it had legalized the Japan Communist Party in 1945. The new Japan Socialist Party returned 92 seats (18% of the vote) in the first postwar election in 1946, and this shot up to 143 seats (28%) in 1947. Hence, by the end of 1947, SCAP began to realize that the danger in postwar Japan was no longer the resurgence of fascism, but rather the rise of communism, and it made a radical reversal in its ambitions in order to confront this new challenge.

The early signs of the so-called 'reverse course' appeared at the start of 1947, when a coalition of labour unions (totalling over 2 million workers) took advantage of their new rights by attempting to organize a general strike. The strike was planned for 1 February, but SCAP stepped in at the last minute and banned the strike on the night of 31 January. For many commentators, this step critically undermined the fledgling labour movement in Japan, and union membership dropped off sharply thereafter (from over 50% to less than 25% of the work force in the 1960s). Union membership remains low to this day, and most are now small-scale 'enterprise unions'.

Very quickly, MacArthur's plans turned from demilitarization and democratization to re-militarization and economic stabilization. The USA now wanted Japan to become its Pacific ally in the global fight against communism. Hence, SCAP instigated a 'Red Purge' that removed 13,000 people from politics and business on the basis that they were 'impeding the goals of the occupation', which had been the same justification used during the purge of the political right. In some cases, the reverse purge literally resulted in the reinstatement of the original wartime occupant of a post. At the same time, MacArthur abandoned his campaign against the *zaibatsu*, which was taking much longer than expected and was seriously damaging the economy. And finally SCAP pushed the Japanese government into establishing its own paramilitary National Police Reserve in 1950, which would eventually form the basis of a more substantial military force: in 1952, it became the National Safety Agency, and then in 1954 the Self-Defence Forces were established, which remains the name of Japan's army, navy, and air force to this day. The question of whether these military forces abrogated (and continue to contravene) Article 9 of the 1947 constitution remains hotly debated today.

The final issue for the occupation forces was the overall health of the Japanese economy. Between 1945 and 1949, inflation had been rampant and out of control, seriously undermining economic and political stability, and raising fears in Washington that the people of Japan would be pushed into the arms of communism. Above all, the capitalist block should build its defence against the communists with a wall of prosperity: a 'crescent of affluence' would contain communist expansion in Asia. The proposed solution was to call in the Detroit banker and auto-executive, Joseph Dodge, to reorganize the economy and attempt to get Japan back on its feet. The so-called 'Dodge Line' was basically an austerity plan, which dramatically cut public spending (abolishing state subsidies and loans, and sacking over 100,000 public employees), decentralized control of foreign currency, and fixed a very favourable exchange rate between the yen and the dollar (360:1) to promote exports. The exchange rate, which increasingly undervalued the yen, was fixed until the 1970s.

Whilst the Dodge Line succeeded in bringing inflation under control, there was every sign that it was going to kill Japan completely. Then, in 1950, Prime Minister Yoshida received a 'gift from the gods': the Korean War. The 'blessed rain from heaven' came in the form of 2 billion dollars' worth of war procurements (which amounted to 60% of Japan's exports over the next three years); exports tripled, production rose by over 70%, and Japan's GNP grew at 12% per annum.

Rather than the Dodge Line, it was the Korean War boom that laid the foundations for Japan's remarkable (even miraculous) economic growth over the next 20 years. At the start of the war, Japan's GNP stood at only 11 billion dollars. By the mid-1950s, it had grown by 250%. By the early 1970s, at over 300 billion, it was the third largest economy in the world (behind the USA and USSR).

14. Prime Minister Yoshida Shigeru

Indeed, Japan's sudden and profound economic growth, combined with the establishment of its 1947 constitution and the beginnings of a military force, meant that the occupation was drawn to a close much earlier than anyone expected. In September 1951, in San Francisco, representatives of 48 nations signed the official peace treaty with Japan, bringing an end to the occupation in April of 1952, just seven years after it had begun. In order to facilitate the rapidity of this move, the USA made separate defence agreements with other key allies in the Asia-Pacific, and also provided for the possibility that Japan's Asian neighbours would be able to negotiate reparation agreements on their own terms afterwards. For Washington, it was important to end the expensive occupation of Japan as quickly as possible, and to establish Japan as a key ally in the hot Cold War in Asia. To this end, only a couple of hours later, Japan and the USA also signed the US–Japan Security Treaty, which continues to tie the USA to the defence of Japan to this day.

For various reasons, the San Francisco Peace Treaty was controversial. A number of nations, including Britain, complained that it was not sufficiently harsh on Japan, and that it should at least have provided for reparation payments to the victims of Japanese imperialism. For the USSR and its European partners, the provision to leave US troops in Japan after the occupation was particularly offensive, and they refused to sign the agreement. And finally, neither China nor Taiwan were even invited to the conference, since it was not yet clear which one would be recognized as 'the one China'. In Japan itself, there were mixed feelings about the terms of the peace. On the one hand, the Japanese were pleased and relieved to be regaining their sovereignty, but it appeared to be only a partial sovereignty, since the USA would retain military bases in Japan and would also keep control over the islands of Okinawa for the foreseeable future (in the end, until 1972). In addition, the US–Japan Security Treaty looked like a double-edged sword, providing a militarily vulnerable Japan with a level of protection, but at the same time implicating Japan in US foreign policy and potentially dragging Japan into other US conflicts. The complexities of this settlement would haunt Japanese foreign policy for many decades.

The economic boom

The early postwar period witnessed incredible change in Japanese society, perhaps paralleled in scale only by the transformations of the early Meiji period. Indeed, the question of Japan's identity in the new world order that was emerging from the wreckage of World War II was just as real and vital as the question had been when Japan had entered the modern world in the 19th century. And a number of the issues were the same: Japan found itself impoverished and at the mercy of the Great Powers of the West, now the superpower of the USA; it found its traditions devastated and a new way of life being urged upon it, with the promise of great riches and power. The parallels were not lost on everyone. For some, the end of the wartime regime and the advent of a pacifistic and democratic constitution represented an opportunity to break with the past and to forge a new Japan. For the majority, struggling to come to terms with what had happened, what had been lost, and what might be gained, there was a complex web of imperatives for continuity with the past and change in the present. For the first time in Japanese history, choices about the future seemed to lie in the hands of the masses themselves. The 1950s and 1960s were culturally and politically volatile decades, even as they were economically miraculous.

In a characteristically pragmatic move, the majority of the people threw themselves into industry to rebuild their nation, whatever it would turn out to be. In the early 1950s, the Japanese government sought to kick-start the process with its first 'rationalization' drive, targeted at the core industries of steel, iron, and coal mining. The metals industry, fed by nearly ¥750 billion, exploded. The amazing growth, which made the ruined postwar Japanese steel industry into the second most profitable in the world before 1959 (behind the USA), was fed not only by the tremendous demand from US forces in Korea but also by the steady influx of new technologies from Europe and the USA. Because Japan did not have to invest in research and development (since ready-made technology could be bought in from outside), growth was rapid.

The growth in the metals industry had a knock-on effect in other industries, such as shipbuilding and (later) automobiles. In terms of shipping, Japan already had a tradition (it was the world's third largest manufacturer in 1935) but its resources had been ruined by the war. Again, partly in response to the demand triggered by the Korean War and partly due to the influx of new technology, Japan was able to rapidly form a new shipbuilding capability. By 1960, Japan was the world's largest shipbuilding nation. By 1975, nearly 50% of the world's new ships were made in Japan.

Many of the giant Japanese car manufacturers started life in this Korean War boom: Nissan, Toyota, and Isuzu all produced vehicles for the US forces, following US designs, but engineered in Japan. Not only did this lead to tremendous growth in the automobile industry, but it also provided Japanese manufacturers with free technology transfer – which would become crucial in the high-growth 1960s. Domestic demand for cars did not really take off until the early 1960s, since per capita income remained low: in 1956, Japan produced only 100,000 vehicles for domestic consumption; by 1963, the figure was 1 million; and in the late 1960s, it was closer to 4 million. By 1967, Japan was the world's second largest car manufacturer.

It was not only the heavy industries that benefited from the economic boom – increasing national wealth had a knock-on effect in other sectors – this was the birth of consumer Japan. Companies like Hitachi and Matsushita Electric started manufacturing washing machines, televisions, and refrigerators – and production of each increased by at least eight times during the late 1950s. Whilst only 1% of homes had televisions in 1956, by 1960 the figure was more than 50%.

If anything, growth in the 1960s was even greater. Prime Minister Ikeda's famous 'income-doubling plan', which was set into motion in 1960, was designed to double Japan's national wealth in 10 years. In fact, this unprecedentedly ambitious plan underestimated the expansion of the Japanese economy – the GNP tripled between 1960 and 1971, representing an average yearly growth rate of 12.1%. By the end of the 1960s, Japan no longer had a balance of payments deficit, which had been acting as a periodic drag on growth up until that point.

However, those who like to talk about an 'economic miracle' should remember that all industrial economies experienced rapid growth during the period from 1950 to 1970. Growth in itself was not unique, although the speed (more than 10% per year) certainly was. Most commentators attribute this 'miracle' to a constellation of very mundane factors: the yen-dollar exchange rate was fixed at 360:1 by the Dodge Line, and it was held artificially at this level until 1971, hence the yen became increasing undervalued, thus stimulating exports; like the rest of the Western world, Japan benefited from a newly liberal trade regime under Bretton Woods and GATT; unlike the rest of the Western world, Japan did not have to spend much of its budget on its military, since it remained sheltered under the US–Japan Security Treaty; as a latecomer amongst the advanced economies, in a liberal trade regime, Japan could buy in new technologies rather than spend time and money on developing them; rapid population growth was accompanied by a tremendous expansion of the education system. Perhaps the most hotly debated 'unique' element in Japanese growth was the role of the bureaucracy and economic management. There is a strong case to be made that the Ministry of International Trade and Industry (MITI) and other ministries (especially the Ministry of Finance, MoF) played a leading role in Japan's rapid growth through a formal and informal *gyôsei shidô* (administrative guidance). However, a simple factor that should not be forgotten was the hard work, industry, and entrepreneurship of the Japanese people themselves. The quip that the 'Japanese work too hard' has a solid basis in reality:

the average Japanese salaryman worked such long hours that they amounted to the equivalent of a full 12 weeks more per year than his European counterparts. In return for this dedication, the large companies offered their employees 'lifetime employment'.

Such rapid growth brought many advantages to the people of Japan: a new middle class emerged rapidly, with common values and aspirations, living in an increasingly suburban world, with paved roads and an extensive train network to help them commute to work. The iconic Shinkansen (bullet-train) went into service as early as 1964, between Tokyo and Osaka, linking the two major commercial cities with unprecedented ease and speed. 1964 was also the year when Tokyo proudly hosted the Olympic Games – a sign that Japan had not only re-entered the international community, but that it was a rich and respectable member of it. In the 1950s, consumers had talked about the 'three treasures' of domestic living (the television, the refrigerator, and the washing machine); by the 1960s, there were three new treasures (an air-conditioner, a car, and a colour television).

By the 1960s, access to the expanded education system was unprecedentedly meritocratic. Gone were the days when access to the elite public universities (the former 'imperial' universities) was determined by social class or financial means; for the first time in its history (and perhaps in the history of the world), the social distribution of entries into the best universities almost exactly matched the demographics of the country as a whole. This was a great testament to the uniform quality and wide availability of primary and secondary schools around the nation. A side-effect of this success was that competition for places at the best universities, particularly Tokyo University itself, was (and remains) incredibly severe. Pre-university students would work even longer hours than their hard-working 'sarariman' fathers, and many (who could afford it) would attend special *gijuku*

15. The Shinkansen bullet-train

(cram schools) to maximize their chances of qualifying for their favoured school. Despite the meritocratic nature of admission to universities (or perhaps because of it), getting in to the right university is of immense importance for a student's career prospects. A graduate of the law faculty at Tokyo University is counted amongst the most elite fraction of her peers, and she has the choice of the top jobs in the government or big business. This 'examination hell' has made the suicide rate in Japanese schools amongst the highest in the world, and the expensive *gijuku* system has reinscribed the privilege of those with higher incomes.

If the great achievements in the sphere of education were accompanied by such serious social problems, so it was also the case that rapid economic development had a much darker side in other areas. Although they were now legally equal to men, women still occupied a different position in society. Just as they had worked for little reward in the textile factories during the war, so in the postwar period they dominated the work force in the electronics factories. Those who worked in offices tended to be employed as 'office lady' assistants and, until a High Court ruling in 1966, they were expected to resign their position once they got married. Progress in gender politics has been slow. Likewise the social discrimination suffered by ethnic minorities (especially the 540,000 Koreans who stayed in Japan after the war) and by social minorities (especially the *burakumin*) continues as a transwar phenomenon. Again, despite laws to protect these groups, sections of society have found ways around these rules.

Economic success also came at the expense of great environmental damage and pollution. The forests of Japan were pushed back into the mountains as the cities expanded to fill the scarce flat ground near the coasts (about 80% of Japan is too mountainous for development). The growth of heavy industry produced vast amounts of poorly regulated chemical waste that poisoned rivers and land. As early as the 1950s, people were complaining of mercury poisoning, which came to be known as Minamata disease after the area effected, and cadmium poisoning, which came to be known as *itai-itai-byô* (literally, 'it really hurts disease') after the symptoms. But it was not until the early 1970s that plaintiffs won any recognition or compensation for their suffering, or that proper environmental regulations were implemented. Thereafter, as its economy stabilized and rode out the oil shocks of the 1970s, Japan gradually became one of the world leaders in environmental protection.

The tribe of the sun

Amidst the rapidly changing material conditions of Japanese society, the people and their culture were also changing. The generation that had been born during the long years of war were turning into young adults in the early 1950s.

They had been deeply impressed by the experience of the US occupation, and the contagion of American culture spread through them rapidly. Not only that, but some of the American disdain for Japan's traditions had rubbed off on them. Youth cultures are rebellious all over the world, and the youth of 1950s Japan had more reason to rebel than most.

Only 14 years after the Imperial Navy attacked Pearl Harbor, a youth movement known as the *taiyô-zoku* (the sun-tribe) emerged in Japan. Its hero was the 24-year-old celebrity playboy Ishihara Shintarô, whose 1955 novel, *Taiyô no kisetsu* (Season of the Sun), set the tone for his fellow youth. The novel, which narrated the story of two brothers sharing a girlfriend, was both a critical success, winning the prestigious Akutagawa Prize, and a popular phenomenon. Only a year later, it had been made into a feature film of the same name. Other novels and movies followed in quick succession, all with the same kinds of themes: the sun-tribe pursued anti-establishment (and sometimes simply pointless) violence and casual morality, endorsing simple brutishness, cynicism, and abandon. Ishihara himself became an idol who seemed to live the life portrayed in his books and films. Like the Teddy Boys in London, the movement had a dress code: for the urban men, stylized 'Shintarô' haircuts and aloha sports clothes, with loose-flowing Byronic shirts, zoot coats, and suede shoes; for the girls, a red-dyed 'mop-top' haircut and toreador pants. Ishihara, still a controversial figure, would go on to become the governor of Tokyo in 1999.

The sun-tribe movement was a symptom of a larger current in Japanese society. It represented a release of tension in the form of (cultural and physical) violence, as popular culture swung towards the political right. The 1950s was a golden period in Japanese cinema, and, following the end of the occupation and its censorship laws, many of the films started to re-consider the events of the war in a distinctly anti-American manner. An early shot in this process was the 1953 film *The Tower of Lilies*, which portrayed young girls committing suicide rather than be captured by the Americans in Okinawa. Kobayashi Masaki's *The Room with Thick Walls* appeared in the same year; it suggested that American conduct during the war had been just as bad as that of the Japanese, and implied that a number of officers had been unjustly punished at the Tokyo Trials. Only one year later, the famous monster epic *Gojira* (Godzilla) was released, telling the story of how a nuclear explosion could have the unintended effect of releasing a giant monster on the world. The 1950s saw dozens of movies about the heroism of Japanese soldiers during the war, about the ways in which the *yakuza* (mafia) had preserved Japan's traditions of honour and martial valour, about samurai, and about monsters.

The politicians were not unaware of this turn in public opinion. In a deliberately ironic reference to MacArthur's famous 'reverse course', future Prime Minister Kishi Nobusuke would refer to a nationalist *gyaku kôsu* (reverse course) in the mid-1950s. Indeed, Kishi himself had been imprisoned as a class A war criminal until 1948, but he was approached by the CIA in 1955 to help unite the conservative factions in Japanese politics into a powerful single party that could ensure the failure of the growing socialist movement. The result, the establishment of the Liberal Democratic Party (LDP) in November 1955 changed the political landscape in Japan forever, inaugurating the so-called '1955 system'; it would remain in power continuously for the next 38 years. The party cultivated close contacts with the former *zaibatsu* and with the permanent bureaucracy, forming a so-called 'iron triangle' that functioned in a distinctly transwar mode. In 1957, Kishi himself became prime minister; just five years after the end of the US occupation (and his legal purge from public office expired).

Kishi's ideological stance was unambiguous. He called for revision of the 1947 constitution (which he argued had been imposed on an unwilling Japan by an occupying force) to permit the rearming of Japan and to declare the emperor the head of state. Should constitutional revision be impossible, Kishi advocated a flexible interpretation of its terms: he suggested that the imperial Rising Sun flag could be reinstated, that the *Kimigayo* national anthem should no longer be banned, that Shintô and traditional Japanese ethics should be more central to Japanese life, and that Japan should become more independent as an international actor (while maintaining a special relationship with the USA).

Kishi did not succeed in pushing all of these measures through the Diet and many of his policies (such as the 1958 Police Bill) met violent opposition from the press, students, and even from his own party. The JCP boycotted debates and tried to barricade the doors of the Diet chambers, while members of the liberal wing of the LDP (led by former prime minister Yoshida Shigeru and future prime ministers Ikeda Hayato and Satô Eisaku, who between them would govern Japan from 1960 until 1972) threatened to resign from the party.

However, the furore over the Police Bill was only a prelude to the greatest political crisis of postwar Japanese history, the so-called *Ampo* or Security Treaty Crisis of 1960. The crisis erupted when Kishi attempted to revise the terms of the US–Japan Security Treaty in time for its renewal. As early as 1958 he started the process of trying to convince the public that Japan needed America's security umbrella, but that it should also seek greater equality within the terms of the treaty, which would mean taking on more responsibility for its own military defence. However, large sections of the public were unconvinced by either assertion, finding both to be in contravention of the pacifist constitution: a coalition of opposition formed the *Ampo jôkai* (National Council against Revision of the Constitution).

Nonetheless, Kishi pressed on, flying to Washington to sign the revised treaty in January 1960. In February, it was presented to the Lower House, but hundreds of separate demonstrations outside, together with cow-walks and filibustering by the opposition parties paralysed the debate. On 19 May, the last day of the parliamentary session, the opposition kidnapped and locked up the speaker of the house to prevent discussion of the treaty, but Kishi called in the police to recover the speaker. He proceeded to exclude the opposition from the Diet chamber and to ratify the treaty himself, with only part of the LDP in attendance, in the middle of the night.

Over the next month, not a single day passed without protests in the streets. On 4 June, 5.5 million people went on strike in protest. On 10 June the Whitehouse press secretary made a visit to Japan to prepare for President Eisenhower's planned visit nine days later. His car was assaulted by demonstrators and he had to be airlifted to safety in a helicopter, while Kishi allegedly called out members of the *yakuza* to control the students. On 15 June, the Upper House received the treaty while a general strike was called and 100,000 protestors did battle with the police and *yakuza* outside the Diet. 17 June: the major newspapers issued a joint editorial warning that the issue at stake was not only pacifism, but that democracy itself was being overthrown. Their words echo those of the powerful public intellectual, Shimizu Ikutarô, for whom the *Ampo* crisis represented the death of democracy in postwar Japan. On 19 June the treaty automatically passed the Upper House, but Eisenhower cancelled his visit. Over the course of the next few weeks, Kishi survived an attempt on his life but resigned his post, and the calmer, less controversial figure of Ikeda Hayato took over.

Identity crisis

Although most famous for his 'income-doubling plan' and for being called a 'transistor salesman' by Charles de Gaulle,

Ikeda was certainly one of the most important prime ministers in the history of postwar Japan. Perhaps his greatest accomplishment was the achievement of a 'politics of patience and reconciliation' that unified the Japanese people behind the project of economic growth. Under Ikeda, the question of Japan's military role was side-lined and society occupied itself with getting rich peacefully.

However, as became apparent in the 1980s, man cannot survive on affluence only, and after the drama of the 1950s, with the sun-tribe a decade older, the question of Japan's national identity was once more on the agenda. At this time, the nation's mood was well reflected in the work of the famous novelist Kawabata Yasunari, who was awarded the *Bunka kunshô* (medal of culture) from the emperor in 1961 and then the Nobel Prize for Literature in 1968 (making him the first Japanese writer to receive it). Kawabata's often beautiful novels have been described as elegies to a lost Japan. Critics often point to *Snow Country* and *Thousand Cranes* as his masterpieces. They contain traditional aesthetics and serve as romantic re-imagings of Japan as a specific type of traditional beauty that is endangered, or at least sullied, by the modern world. Indeed, Kawabata appears to have thought of himself as a conduit through which traditional Japanese culture could be preserved and transmitted to the postwar generations. Furthermore, Kawabata's work was easily palatable for an international audience, since it represented Japan in an exotic and unthreatening way that appealed to Western audiences. The 1950s and 1960s saw many of his novels translated into English, and ironically his international fame was part of the reason for his domestic fame. The contrast with Ishihara's work in the 1950s could not be more stark.

An indication of the way in which attitudes had changed towards a Japanese identity that rested upon martial valour and violence is the case of Kawabata's contemporary and friend, the writer Mishima Yukio. Mishima had shot to fame in the 1950s after a

16. The novelist Kawabata Yasunari

series of astonishing and complex novels, such as *Temple of the Golden Pavilion*, *Forbidden Colours*, and *Confessions of a Mask*. He dealt with daring themes, such as homosexuality and the relationship between sex and violence. As the 1950s drew on, Mishima became increasingly interested in his body and the martial arts; he took up body-building, kendô, and boxing, and started to present himself in the manner of a movie star. In hindsight, various biographers have wondered whether this was the onset of some form of masochistic, narcissistic disorder.

Like Kawabata, Mishima also believed that his life and work should somehow represent Japan. However, whilst the two great novelists shared a delicate sense of beauty, their visions of Japan were radically different. For Mishima, the *Ampo* was a real turning point. Rather than representing the end of a problematic and violent decade that risked undermining Japanese democracy – which was the realization that encouraged many readers to turn to Kawabata – Mishima was mostly concerned with the way that Japanese society had recoiled from Kishi's vision of Japan as a land of martial valour. Immediately following the crisis, Mishima published a little volume called *Patriotism*, in which he set out what he thought it should mean to love Japan. His next works, *The Sword* and *Sun and Steel*, were devoted to explorations of the aesthetics of violence, and he announced that the goal of his life was to acquire the characteristics of a true Japanese warrior – *bunburyôdô* (the way of the warrior and the scholar combined). At about the same time, his book *Patriotism* was made into a film, produced and starred in by Mishima himself.

So great was his fame that when he requested special permission to train with the *Jieitai* (the Self Defence Forces) from his friend Prime Minister Satô, he was granted it. At the same time, the literary establishment started to distance itself from his views. In interviews he spoke about the tragedy that the emperor had been forced to renounce his divinity after the war, and asserted that the wartime *kokutai* (national polity) had been the authentic Japan – the Americans had emasculated the country and ruined its spirit. He argued that the postwar period had left the Japanese confused about their values, and that this was the perfect time to revive the traditional Japanese ideal of *bushidô* (the way of the warrior). Finally, in 1967 he founded a secret, paramilitary society called the *Tatenokai* (the Shield Society). Prime Minister

Satô even gave Mishima some funds to help run the group, and future prime minister Nakasone Yasuhiro, then defence agency chief, granted the *Tatenokai* free access to all *Jieitai* facilities in Japan in 1970.

Meanwhile, anti-Vietnam War demonstrations pulsed around Japan's cities, overflowing into peace rallies, and running parallel to student activism. In the spring of 1969, many university campuses were closed down because of student protests about Vietnam, about *Ampo*, and about tuition fees. On the campus of Tokyo University, the protests were violent and a number of professors were literally held hostage and interrogated in lecture halls, including the eminent political scientist Maruyama Masao. Excited by the activism, Mishima visited the students in Tokyo, but was disappointed by their motives.

On 25 November 1970, Mishima and a group of *Tatenokai* infiltrated a military base in Tokyo and took General Mashita Kanetoshi hostage, while Mishima himself stood out on the balcony to speak to the assembled troops. He told the *Jieitai* that the real Japan had been killed by talk of liberty and democracy, that the emperor had been humiliated by the Americans, and that they – the military – held the future of Japan in their hands. As an example of the weakness and ignorance of the politicians, he stated that the *Jieitai* should have been sent in against the student demonstrators at Tokyo University in the previous year (instead of the riot police).

His dramatic speech received no response from the troops, who could barely hear him. Then he returned to the general's office, where he committed *seppuku* in the traditional way and killed himself, apparently because he could not live in a Japan that had been so polluted and compromised by Western modernity.

It must be said that Mishima was an extreme case, and that neither his actions nor his views elicited much support in Japan.

17. Mishima Yukio, delivering his speech to the military from the balcony

Indeed, the overall reaction appears to have been one of
incomprehension. Prime Minister Satô, Mishima's friend and
benefactor, was reputed to have responded that he assumed that
Mishima had gone insane. And Mishima remains a controversial
figure to this day. However, the existence of a cultural space
between Kawabata (who also committed suicide a couple of years
later) and Mishima serves to indicate the dimensions of Japan's

identity crisis throughout the 1960s and 1970s. Both called for a return to traditional Japanese values amidst rapid economic development and the creation of a consumer society, but they could not agree on what those values might be.

Bubbling into postmodernity

Elsewhere in the world, the miraculous growth of the Japanese economy was exciting a range of reactions. While the rest of the planet laboured under stagflation, recession, and unemployment in the wake of the oil shocks of 1973 and 1978, the Japanese economy continued to grow through the 1980s at about 5% per annum – it had weathered the 1970s through a combination of exploiting the elasticity of its so-called 'dual economy', industrial restructuring (away from heavier industries), energy diversification, and creative off-shoring. At the end of the 1980s, the Tokyo stockmarket was worth 40% of the world's market; land prices in Japan were ludicrously high (for a while the land under the city of Tokyo was worth more than Canada). At one extreme, Japan was represented as a threatening global monster that was intent on forging a massive postwar empire, simply substituting yen for the bullets of the co-prosperity sphere: the phenomenon of 'Japan bashing' became commonplace in the USA. At the other extreme, Japan was seen as a mystical and inspiring model for economic development, and a range of populist books were published that claimed to unlock the secret connections between Japanese work ethics, Confucian organization, the spirit of *bushidô*, and business success. The world clamoured around the invented image of the salaryman-samurai.

Meanwhile, in Japan, despite claims that the vast majority of the population was now a homogeneous middle class with shared life-goals and equal access to the resources of an affluent state, the Japanese society that entered the 1980s and 1990s was still unsure of its place in the world. The *Nihonjinron* industry boomed, as the Japanese population consumed hundreds of treatises that sought to explain the uniqueness of the Japanese people from ethnic, psychological, sociological, and religious perspectives. The new generation came to be called a new species (*shin jinrui*). They were confident and proud of Japan's affluence, but never having known the hardships of the previous generation, they were complacent about the wealth. The banks made casual loans: very famously the Industrial Bank of Japan lent an Osaka woman 2 billion dollars against a small chain of restaurants, which she proceeded to lose on the stockmarket after taking financial advice from her psychic. In the end, it turned out that she had faked the ownership deeds on the restaurants. Corruption in business and politics seemed to be growing, and the people lost faith in their politicians after the drama of the Lockheed Scandal in 1985 and then the Recruit Scandal in 1988, the repercussions of which would contribute to the brief fall from power of the LDP in 1993, for the first time since its establishment in 1955.

This 'new species' of Japanese citizen was not content to quietly and selflessly dedicate its life to Japan's economic growth, and it complained about the long hours of work and the lack of time to enjoy the spoils of Japan's affluence. The term *karôshi* (death from overwork) became a commonplace, and emergency hotlines were even established to try to prevent the overworked from breaking down or committing suicide. At the same time, the previous generations complained that the 'new species' had lost all social consciousness and discipline, the characteristics that had defined their postwar identities.

Instead of dedicating themselves to a single company in 'lifetime employment' arrangements, the new species were increasingly *furitaa*, seeking freelance work with a sequence of employers to enable them to travel and to fit their work around the demands of the rest of their lives. This emphasis on leisure and ways of forming identities that were not dependent upon work found expression in the creation of multiple 'micro-masses' or subcultures: office ladies and college girls adopted a new form of the '*moga*' (modern girl), defining a subculture in terms of rampant consumerism, and building their identities amidst designer handbags, European shoes, and stylized haircuts. In the 1990s, this movement became associated with the phenomenon of *enjo kôsai*, 'compensated dating', which labelled the practice of young girls (often of school age) dating older men in return for being bought the latest consumer goods. Although, in general, the *moga* was a leisure-time identity: at work or in school, the same *moga* would present themselves impeccably in their uniforms. This subculture and its moral experimentation is captured in the work of authors such as Yoshimoto Banana, whose name is deliberately as ludicrous in Japanese as in English.

Alongside the *moga* were other subcultures, such as the iconic '*otaku*' (geek): usually young men who became obsessively interested in one topic or another – frequently 'anti-social' activities such as computer games, anime, or manga, which the *otaku* would collect in vast numbers, perhaps spending the weekend engaged in 'cosplay' reconstructions of their favourite characters.

The development of these new consumerist subcultures touched off what some have referred to as the '*otaku* panic'. Despite evidence that the *moga* and the *otaku* continued to function in their jobs and continued to work longer hours than nearly every other society on the planet (with the exception of South Korea), critics argued that these micro-masses demonstrated the 'hollowing out' of Japanese society and culture. The older generations feared for the moral and cultural collapse of their nation. A conservative drive to preserve a more traditional Japan emphasized the need for people to get out of the sprawling urban centres and to 'discover Japan' by visiting rural areas, which were still less transformed by the postwar boom. This nostalgia and romanticization of the countryside was accompanied by genuine growth in domestic tourism.

However, for creative intellectuals such as Yoshimoto Takaaki (the father of Banana), these social movements revealed that Japanese society was moving through modernity and out the other side, into a postmodern condition in which individuals were no longer slaves to the material expectations of their society, but in which they were free to define the meaning of their lives for themselves. Postmodern Japan was about individual people, and not about Japan at all.

This mood was captured in the work of the world-famous novelist Murakami Haruki, whose important duology, *A Wild Sheep Chase* and *Dance, Dance, Dance* provided bookends for the 1980s. One of the central themes of these best-selling,

18. **The neon lights of Shinjuku, Tokyo**

postmodern novels is the way in which individuality is consistently destroyed by the homogenizing imperatives of the system itself. For instance, the eponymous 'sheep' is a sinister presence that inhabits the minds of people like a supernatural parasite and gradually eliminates its host's personality, replacing it with its own; the host enjoys a sense of power and comfort that accompanies this possession, and in particular comes to feel free of any sense of responsibility for his/her actions. As a critique of the totalizing national culture that Murakami and others perceived in Japan, the sheep is a powerful symbol. At some point all the possessed characters must choose whether to surrender the last vestiges of their personalities to the sheep, or to fight it and expel it. Those who choose the latter become tragic figures: they go insane or commit suicide, while the sheep simply moves on to someone else. In one interpretation, the micro-masses of the 1980s and 1990s appear to be fighting the sheep. In another, the sheep is not conservative Japanese culture, but rather commercialism itself, in which case the micro-masses are as possessed by it as anyone else. There is no escape.

This feeling of despair became characteristic of the so-called 'lost decade' of the 1990s, after the collapse of the bubble economy and the death of the Shôwa emperor in 1989. Unable to sustain the artificially inflated and over-confident economy, the stockmarket crashed and Japan's cultural confidence was dented. Despite remaining the world's second largest economy and running trade surpluses with nearly all of its trading partners, society's faith in the sheep and in the politicians (already shaky amidst the corruption scandals of the 1980s) was shattered. At the same time, with the end of the Cold War, there was unprecedented international pressure on Japan to take a more active and leading role in world affairs: Japan's indecisive (and entirely financial) response to the First Gulf War in 1991 only served to underline the fact that Japan had still not come to terms with a coherent postwar identity.

The mid-1990s saw a succession of crises that triggered deeper self-reflection about Japan's identity and role. If the place of Japan in the US-led world order was brought into question during the Gulf War, this question became painfully personalized in 1995 when three US servicemen kidnapped and raped a 12-year-old Okinawan girl. This incident restarted the perennial debate about why the USA should still be allowed to maintain bases in Japan, now that Japan was a powerful country in its own right. In the same year, a group of revisionist intellectuals started the *Liberal View of History Group*, which sought to revise society's perception of Japan's 20th-century history in a way that would allow the Japanese to be proud of its ambitions and conduct during the Great East Asia War. For some, such as the influential writer and critic Katô Norihiro, Japan's treatment of its past and its identity bordered on being pathological: under pressure from the USA in the postwar period, Japanese society had become sick, masochistic, and schizophrenic – what was needed was a frank discussion about what Japan's *real* identity was.

However, two other crises in the same year shook Japan even more. In January of 1995 a massive earthquake that killed over 6,000 people and left 300,000 homes in ruins hit the city of Kobe. And then, on 20 March, the religious cult *Aum Shinrikyô* launched the infamous sarin gas attacks on the Tokyo underground, killing 12 people and injuring more than 5,000.

The people of Japan were stunned by the sequence of events, and the inefficient responses of the government further undermined public confidence in the establishment. Murakami Haruki attempted to give reason to the madness in two short books about the events. In *After the Quake*, he provides a cluster of short stories that discuss possible causes of the earthquake: was it a natural disaster in the 'end times' to punish Japan for the frivolities of the 1980s? Was it caused by moral decay – by the jealousy of a married women whose husband was cheating on her? Or was it caused by the awakening of a giant worm under the city that had been feeding on greed and hate for several decades?

In *Underground* (his first work of non-fiction), Murakami asks how can we explain the *Aum* phenomenon and how it can be used to understand the woes of the rest of the society. He argues that anyone who doubts the existence of a serious philosophical and spiritual gap in contemporary Japan has not really considered the true significance of 20 March 1995:

> The reality is that beneath the main system of Japanese society there exists no subsystem, no safety net, to catch those who slip through the cracks. This reality has not changed as a result of the incident. There is a basic gap in our society, a kind of black hole, and no matter how thoroughly we stamp out the Aum Shinrikyô cult, similar groups are sure to form in the future to bring about the same kinds of disasters.

The *Aum* group wanted to take control of Tokyo (and then the world) in order to eradicate the spiritual decay that had been caused by Western material values – by modernity. The new world would be led by psychically gifted people (rather than materially powerful people), who would be ranked like characters in the RPG *Dungeons and Dragons*. The most powerful of these claimed to have caused the Kobe earthquake. One of the things that most shocked Japanese society was that the membership of the group was not exclusively anti-social *otaku* or the uneducated, indeed the membership included many gifted scientists and business leaders. Why were such brilliant and talented people driven into this kind of organization?

For Murakami, the answer was clear: modern Japan was failing to provide a coherent sense of identity and community for its people. At the turn of the 21st century, *Aum* was like a nation inside the nation: a sub-nation that captured the imagination of the disillusioned – it was an alternative present (of the kind that society had feared that the *otakus* lived in) which was supposed to eliminate the woes of the actual present.

In June 1997, Murakami's diagnosis seemed to be further vindicated when a 14-year-old boy decapitated an 11-year-old and dumped his body in front of their school. He committed two murders and a host of other attempts, and his diaries showed that this was a 'game' with the authorities, that it was 'revenge' against the school system for making him 'a transparent being'. He had even made up a god, Bamoidooki, to whom he had sacrificed escalating levels of life.

Of course, these micro-masses are subcultural movements in Japan rather than the mainstream. However, concern about them and about what they say about Japan's ongoing crisis of identity, and its problematic relationship with the modern, is one of the characteristics of society more widely. As Japan moves through the 21st century, the challenge to answer the question of what it means to be modern in modern Japan remains.

Chapter 5
Overcoming denial: contemporary Japan's quest for normalcy

What is a normal Japan?

Japan's engagement with the question of its identity during the Cold War was somewhat introspective, as it struggled to come to terms with the consequences of its attempts to 'overcome modernity' and its defeat in the Pacific War. However, the 1990s saw Japan emerge from beneath its sheltered position under the US umbrella and throw itself into the new post-Cold War international system. Whilst it would certainly be an exaggeration to compare the early 1990s with the mid-1850s, there is some leverage to be gained from the idea that Japan affected genuine shifts in perspective at both times: from largely domestic issues to concerns about Japan's identity and role in a new world order. Indeed, in both cases, Japan was pulled out of its interiority by the twin demands of the USA and the imperatives of the emerging international society: in 1854, by Perry's 'black ships' and the imperial trade regimes, and in 1991 by President George Bush's pressure on Japan to contribute troops to the UN-sanctioned force in Kuwait. In both cases, Japan's response to this external pressure (or *gaiatsu*) was conflicted, uncertain, and slow, as decision-makers and the public debated how and whether Japan should take up its new responsibilities on the international stage. In 1991, under tremendous pressure, Japan prevaricated and then sent 13 billion dollars instead of personnel.

Since 1947, Japan's foreign policy had been tame and low profile, and its orientation towards security issues had been guided by the famous 'peace clause' (Article 9) of its constitution, which meant that it had not engaged in any significant military activity and was ostensibly forbidden from doing so. The US–Japan Security Treaty had effectively insulated Japan from the need to think too seriously about its role in the 'high politics' of the international system.

The combination of Japan's 'peace constitution', its US-tutelage, and its so-called 'nuclear allergy', which followed on from the horrific experience of being the world's first and only victims of atomic bombings, fed into a dominant discourse of 'anti-militarism', or even pacifism, in the postwar period. On the international stage, Japan had sought to represent itself as an icon of 'civilian' or 'merchant' power, self-consciously and deliberately eschewing the trappings of military, Great Power status. For Japan's neighbours, who were understandably wary of a re-armed Japan, this had been good news throughout the Cold War. However, regional criticisms of Japan's 'pacifistic' identity became increasingly prevalent through the 1970s and 1980s, as Japan's economy bubbled to an astonishing size: pacifism and the nuclear allergy began to look like alibis that sought to transform Japan into a victim of its own history of aggression, hence alleviating the need for it to apologize to its neighbours for its conduct in the first half of the 20th century.

In other words, the early 1990s brought the question of Japan's international identity into sharp relief: was Japan really a pacifist polity that consciously chose to avoid military resolutions to international problems, or was this appearance merely a side-effect of the US occupation and then the US–Japan Security Treaty? An important issue within Japan itself, which was voiced powerfully by the influential politician Ôzawa Ichirô, was whether Japan's apparent anti-militarism actually made it an aberration in the modern world. In his *Blueprint for a New Japan* (1994), Ôzawa famously called on Japan to finally rid itself of its 'postwar mentality' and its preoccupation with the legacy of the Pacific War, and to become a 'normal country'. By this, he meant a country that could take on responsibilities in the international system that were commensurate with its economic status. A popular and emotive example was the claim that Japan, as the second most generous contributor to the United Nations, should have a permanent seat on the UN Security Council. In concrete terms, he wanted Japan to revise its constitution to enable the overseas despatch of the Self Defence Forces as part of UN peace-keeping operations or other mechanisms of international security. In fact, Ôzawa was one of the chief architects of the 1992 International Peace Cooperation Law, which finally made provision for the (limited) participation of the SDFs in UN peace-keeping operations, albeit too late for the first Gulf War. Japan's first mission under this law was to Cambodia in 1992.

The question of Japan's international 'normalcy' has been pervasive in politics, society, and culture since the early 1990s, and it remains unresolved to this day. For some commentators, the problem can usefully be phrased in terms of Japan's twin deficits: first, in terms of the absence of 'normal' capabilities (that is, a powerful military together with legal mechanisms, and social will, to employ it); and second, in terms of the absence of 'normal' legitimacy in the international system (that is, the apparent failure of Japan to 'come to terms with its past' and to apologize to its neighbours).

In fact, Japan's capability deficit is something of an illusion. It's Self Defence Forces are amongst the most technologically advanced military forces in the world. Whilst Japan maintains a strict 'non-nuclear' armaments policy, it has long had the

19. Air-SDF F-15 refuelling

necessary technology to construct such weapons, and also a
space programme with the necessary delivery technologies. It is
true that Japan lacks the capability to project an invasion force
overseas, but its defensive capacities are second to none, and it
has a range of 'over the horizon' technologies that would
facilitate pre-emptive strikes at the Asian mainland. In brief,
despite the small size of its SDFs (in terms of personnel and
percentage of GDP spent, less than 1%), Japan's 'non-military'
is one of the most formidable in the Asia region.

In other words, the real sources of Japan's 'capability deficit' are
legal and cultural rather than material, and since Prime Minister
Koizumi's enactment of the Anti-Terrorism Specials Measures
Law (2001), which enabled the SDFs to be deployed in support
of US forces in Afghanistan and Iraq during the second Gulf War,
the legal barriers to Japan's military actions have been severely
diluted. Indeed, the discrepancy between Japan's flexible
interpretation of its 'peace constitution' and the letter of Article 9
has led many to demand the revision of the constitution itself,
to bring it in line with reality. This type of criticism often

leads to cynical accusations that Japan's ostensible 'pacifism' has more to do with public relations than substance, and that Japan is clinging to its self-constructed image as a victim of World War II for its own advantage.

This brings us to the question of Japan's 'legitimacy deficit', which has been a central, volatile, and pervasive issue since the 1990s until the present day. In many ways, it boils down to the accusation that Japan and the Japanese are somehow in denial about their own history, or that they have not 'come to terms with their past' because of their privileged position under US patronage during the Cold War. Hence, the end of the Cold War provided an occasion for exposing, and hopefully addressing, this problem, which effectively ties the legitimacy of Japan's contemporary international role to the question of its ability to examine its responsibility for the Pacific War. Because this issue is so central to the themes of identity and modernity, and because it remains a 'living issue' for contemporary Japan, we should spend some time on it here.

The legitimacy deficit and the question of war responsibility

The heart of this problem is the resilient presumption amongst various commentators and practitioners that whilst Germany (and the Germans) appear to have made peace with (and shown penitence for) the violence perpetrated by them in World War II, Japan (and the Japanese) have not.

Interestingly, however, Japan has been one of the most prolific issuers of apologies and enactors of atonement throughout the 1990s, a period characterized by what Wole Soyinka has called the global *fin de millenaire* fever for atonement', starting with the controversial statement by the then new Emperor Akihito (and then Prime Minister Kaifu) to RoK President Roh Tae Woo during his visit to Japan in 1990, through Prime Minister

Murayama's elaborate statement on the 50th anniversary of Japan's defeat (1995), and to Prime Minister Obuchi's written apology (for abuses perpetrated during the occupation of Korea) to RoK President Kim Dae Jung in October 1998.

Despite these significant and substantial developments, both in the international discourse of penitence and reconciliation (after the Truth and Reconciliation Commission in South Africa, 1995) *and* in the conduct of Japan, the impression that Japan has not yet demonstrated (or perhaps even experienced) sufficient penitence remains. So, how can we understand the resilience of this view in the light of so much evidence to the contrary?

The simplest political answer to this question is merely to shift its terms and to suggest that the problem does not lie in Japan at all, but rather in the refusal of Japan's neighbours to accept Japanese penitence and move on. The cynic could make a simple argument about the economic and political benefits that accrue to the PRC or RoK for as long as they refuse to acknowledge that Japan has finally emerged from the long postwar period. This is certainly an interpretation of PRC and RoK motives that can be heard in some segments of Japanese opinion today.

A more Japan-centred answer revolves around the question of what penitence actually means. Here, a cynic might voice the commonplace objection that Japan has apologized many times, *but it has never really meant it.* That is, Japanese apologies have been entirely political acts, and not penitent in any moral sense at all; they are insincere in some way. For this hypothetical (yet pervasive and familiar) cynic, Japanese apologies are not attempts to ask for forgiveness – they are not a humbling before the wronged of history – they are simply an expedient way to push into the future.

Leaving aside (for the moment at least) the slightly troubling implications of the personification of the nation-state in this psychologically informed critique, and also leaving aside the simple repost that 'of course Japan's apologies are political acts because Japan is a state (not a person) and all acts of state are political', this view of Japanese penitence as a type of 'role-playing game' does provide us with some theoretical leverage on the problem. In particular, there was a lively public discourse in the mid to late 1990s that also formulated the problem in these problematically psychological terms.

Denial as national pathology and the 'lost decade' of the 1990s

In many ways, the global *'fin de millenaire* fever for atonement' was a fever for truth-telling, sincerity, and historical revelations, aimed at an exorcism of the demons of history. It seemed to rest upon the Freudian idea that a repressed past left 'indelible scars' on the collective unconsciousness, concealing infected wounds that had to be cleansed for the good of the body politic. One interesting aspect of this view is that it is underpinned by a modernist idea of the unitary self, in which persistent denial is interpreted as pathological (personality splitting) or politically atrophic (cultural amnesia). For various reasons, this idea of the self (or especially of the nation) is highly dubious, especially in a global context.

However, as early as the 1970s in Japan the psychologist Kishida Shû theorized modern Japan's condition as schizophrenic. In the 1990s, Kishida's view was adopted by the controversial and highly influential intellectual Katô Norihiro, who similarly 'diagnosed' Japan's postwar 'illness' as that of schizophrenia, arguing powerfully that Japan's 'personality' really had been splintered into an inner and outer self by the contradictions inherent in the US occupation of Japan after the war. For him, postwar Japan had been placed in an impossible position, between the need to become democratic and the realization that democracy was being imposed by the former enemy. The result of this dilemma, which he expresses in his famous book *Nihon no mushisô* (Japan's

Thoughtlessness, 1999), is that the 'public Japan' accepted the desires and directives of the USA (notably pacifism and democracy) as its own, whilst the 'private Japan' maintained a divergent and often contradictorily nationalistic self-image with some elements of continuity with the imperial period.

Katô suggests that whilst this 'splintering' solution might have been rational and efficacious (that is, it enabled Japan to prosper under the US umbrella during the Cold War period), the costs for Japan have been huge: postwar Japan has become mentally ill. In his landmark essay, *Haisengo-ron* (On Post-Defeat, 1997), Katô kick-started the most serious and important intellectual debate of the 1990s in Japan, the so-called *rekishi shutai ronsô* (the debate over the historical subject). In it, Katô argued that Japan's schizophrenia may have been rational and explicable during the Cold War when it was dependent on the good graces of the USA, but that it was now well past the time to diagnose and cure the illness that had afflicted Japan for the last 50 years. According to Katô, Japan's schizophrenic condition had prevented postwar Japan from fully developing a coherent and modern historical subjectivity with which it could face its own wartime past – neither the public Japan (which was forced to condemn its own history in a blanket fashion because of its US orientation) nor private Japan (which existed in the reactive, nationalist shadows out of the light) had been able to negotiate honestly or wholly with the actual events of Japan's past, including the atrocities committed by it during the war.

The task of the historical subject debate, then, was to find a way to construct a modern, authentic, unitary, non-pathological national subject that would be able to take responsibility for its own historical transgressions. There is a clear echo here of the so-called *shutaisei* (subjectivity) debates between Maruyama Masao and the early postwar Marxists, in which Maruyama argued influentially and powerfully that the absence of a properly developed sense of modern subjectivity (and in particular the absence of an active public sphere in which this subjectivity could participate) had prevented the wartime Japanese from understanding their responsibility to resist the imperial state. For Maruyama, this had led to a 'system of irresponsibilities' that had permitted Japan to 'slither into war' without any sense of control or responsibility for its actions. For him, already in 1946, the most vital task for postwar Japan was to develop a modern sense of subjectivity (*shutaisei*) that properly and responsibly connected public and private. Without this, Japanese democracy would never become anything more than a superficial, institutional veneer.

Katô's controversial position in the 1990s suggests that Japanese penitence in the postwar has indeed been inauthentic in a number of very important (and rather fundamental) ways: public penitence by Japan has been merely an aspect of its adopted, 'US-friendly', politically correct personality. Rather than being a highpoint of the expression of sincere penitence during the '*fin de millenaire* fever for atonement', the 1990s represent a real (even clinical) crisis of disingenuousness.

It is somewhat unfortunate that Katô's *rekishi shutai ronsô* coincided almost perfectly with the emergence of a group of right-wing historical revisionists, including Fujioka Nobukatsu (author of the 1997 book *Kyokasho ga oshienai rekishi* (History Not Taught in Textbooks)) and the manga artist Kobayashi Yoshinori (author of the *Shin-gômanism* or *New Arogantism* series). Superficially, this group's agenda appears to point towards the same issue – the need for a new *Nihon jishin no rekishi-ishiki* (distinct Japanese historical consciousness). However, whilst Katô called for a genuine (if controversial) engagement with Japan's darkest and most shameful moments (albeit via an open reappraisal of *Japan's own suffering* during, and sense of trauma about, that period), Fujioka and Kobayashi were (and remain) rather more concerned with revising World War II into something for which the Japanese should be proud.

Japan's neighbours, as well as large segments of Japan's own population, are understandably sensitive to such moves.

A related issue here regards the frequent and proximal charge that Japan's penitence cannot be sincere because of the very public acts of alleged nationalism performed by high-profile political figures. Here we are talking about the official recognition of the *nisshôki* (Rising Sun flag) and *kimigayo* (the national anthem) in 1999 by Prime Minister Obuchi; the infamous visits to Yasukuni shrine by former Prime Minister Koizumi and his attempts to reform the supposedly 'un-Japanese' Fundamental Law of Education (1947) to provide for patriotism classes in school; or former Prime Minister Abe's involvement with historically revisionist school textbooks and his call for revision of Article 9 to permit (or legitimate) Japanese rearmament.

A crucial issue that governs the reception of these moments is whether or not they constitute public acts of state or the private acts of a Japanese citizen. It is significant, therefore, that since Prime Minister Nakasone in the 1980s, Japanese politicians have always insisted, for instance, that they visit Yasukuni shrine *as private Japanese citizens*, not in their public, political capacities. In fact, we might see the gradual blurring of this inner/outer personality distinction (for example, Koizumi Jun'ichirô, *as prime minister*, visited Yasukuni *publicly as a private citizen*) as being part of a genuine process of engagement with the schizophrenia thesis itself. In other words, visiting Yasukuni and calling for public debate on the meaning of patriotism and its place in national education and so on might actually be seen as *therapy*: might these visits be deliberate attempts to confront the problem and to resolve the so-called 'personality splitting' that was irresolvable during the Cold War? Could they be seen as attempts to construct the kind of public space for genuine, responsible discourse that Katô (and Maruyama before him) found to be critically absent from postwar Japan? Rather than

20. Former Prime Minister Koizumi visits the Yasukuni shrine, 15 August 2006

being a romantic or militarist call for the imperial past, is this not simply a mechanism to mediate the construction of a *Nihon jishin no rekishi-ishiki*, and to involve private persons in public spaces – to make the Japanese participate in their postwar state as political and historical subjects?

What is particularly fascinating about this type of argument, controversial as it may be, is that it draws in a cluster of fundamental and profound concepts into complex interdependence: we can see numerous ways in which questions of postwar penitence, democracy, modernity, and subjectivity interpenetrate in contemporary Japan. The idea of political pathology in this case rests upon the assumption of the normalcy (and health) of a unitary, modern self at both the individual and national levels. It is an open question at this stage whether we might more profitably view Japan as a 'postmodern' state.

Can 'Japan' receive therapy?

Something that becomes very clear about the terms of this debate is that they are phrased in the language of a therapeutic paradigm that pathologizes national action. The nation is treated as a sick individual: split by the trauma of its history/memory, Japan retreated into a state of denial, where it paradoxically knows and does not know the horrors of its past. Of course, this paradox (of not knowing what you know) is central to the nature of denial, since one cannot deny something that one does not (at least on some level and with a certain level of suspicion) know.

Yet, the question remains: are nations sufficiently like people for this to make any sense? Do nations, like individual people, have psyches? Can a nation's past make its people ill, in the same way as repressed memories can make individuals ill? Most commentators seem to agree that these psychological concepts *cannot* simply be transposed to the political level.

An individual's suffering and psychological trauma is of an entirely different order from national suffering and political trauma.

In other words, this kind of discourse appears to be a trick. Nations are not people and talking about them as though they are represents (deliberately or otherwise) a shifting of the political landscape. Indeed, this therapeutic mode of thinking is essentially self-referential. It turns attention away from the subjects or victims of past aggressions and transforms the perpetrator into the patient. In other words, rather than being concerned with the suffering inflicted on others at the moment that originated the pathology (in Japan's case, the Pacific War), the concern is for the psychological suffering of the patient as a result of not being able to deal with the memory of that event or period. As a response to trauma, this is a pathology of denial.

From this perspective, the meaning and significance of 'coming to terms with the past', or even feeling penitence for it, shifts: it is no longer about seeking forgiveness from those who were wronged or about humbling yourself before them and granting them power over you (that is, the power of forgiveness) – indeed, it is not about them at all – but rather it is about healing and transforming yourself.

In other words, the popular and influential schizophrenia thesis regarding the inauthenticity of Japan's postwar penitence actually inverts the historical and moral issue, transforming Japan into the principal victim of World War II and making the subsequent attempts to come to terms with that war into efforts to heal and rebuild Japan itself. Critics, both inside and outside Japan, have been quick to point out that this image is sustained by Japan's persistent reluctance to formally acknowledge (or pay reparations to) the so-called 'comfort women', largely Korean and Chinese women who were exploited as the 'sex slaves' of the Imperial Army.

21. Protestors in Seoul act out the decapitation of Prime Minister Koizumi, following Koizumi's visit to Yasukuni

These kinds of therapeutic narratives privilege modernist assumptions of unitary selfhood, feeding into ongoing debates about Japan's complicated relationship with modernity and its overcoming. Indeed, one of Katô Norihiro's most controversial assertions has been that Japan needs to mourn its 3 million war dead before it can grieve for (or properly express responsibility for) Asia's 20 million dead. The idea is that Japanese society should reach a unified consensus on its own sense of self and historical consciousness before it can enact meaningful apologies as a (psychically) healthy and integrated, modern agent.

Consequences of illegitimacy

Since the end of the Cold War, the importance of addressing this legitimacy deficit has increased dramatically. Many of Japan's attempts to develop a leadership role in the region have been undermined by the persistent suspicion that its imperial ambitions remain unreconstructed: Japan's tentative role in regional security apparatus, such the ASEAN Regional Forum (established in 1994), or Prime Minister Hashimoto's abortive attempts to form a regional economic block to break the Asian financial crisis (1997), might serve as examples. In general, East Asia has been unable or unwilling to develop the kinds of regional apparatus found in Europe.

Nonetheless, Japan has been innovative in developing non-military security mechanisms, partially as a way to guarantee its own security without testing the parameters of Article 9, partly out of the hope that focusing on such measures would boost regional confidence in its intentions, and partially out of a sincere concern for broader issues of 'human security' in the contemporary world. In particular, as the Japanese economy has grown, Tokyo has attempted to develop a 'Comprehensive Security' platform. The phrase was coined by Prime Minister Ôhira in 1978, and was quickly adopted as a slogan for the Satô-Reagan partnership in 1981: Comprehensive Security for the Free World! The concept of comprehensive security broadens the notion of threat from being simply military to include other factors, such as the environment, poverty, and famine. It has also grown to encompass the idea of 'human security', defined as freedom from fear (defined in juxtaposition to the notion of human rights and freedom from want).

The Japanese government has pursued these ideals with various policy mechanisms, including the generous provision of Official Development Assistance (ODA), the vast majority of which has been dispersed to its Asian neighbours. After 1989, Japan became the world's largest donor of ODA. However, it has met with criticism from segments of the international community for a number of reasons: during the Cold War, Japan was sometimes criticized for distributing tied-ODA instead of war reparations to its neighbours; it has been accused of inconsistent distribution of the aid; or sometimes for attempting to use the aid as a form of economic imperialism. In response to these criticisms, Japan passed a comprehensive ODA bill in 1992 that clearly spelled out the basis of its distribution, tying its ODA distribution to the concepts of comprehensive and human security, and the promotion of democracy and human rights.

Nonetheless, there remain critics in East Asia who see all of Japan's efforts at regional confidence-building and comprehensive security as little more than confidence tricks. Wherever they see the yen, they see the covert insinuation of a new kind of Japanese empire, sold to the world in the form of financial aid, Nissan cars, Sony Playstations. Sensitive to such fears, the Ministry of Foreign Affairs has taken the question of image very seriously. In 2007, it launched the 'Creative Japan' campaign, in which it represented Japan as the home of artistic innovation and pop-culture phenomena, naming anime, manga, and video games, along with food, fashion, and architecture, as amongst its primary contributions to world culture. Unlike the USA, however, which has managed to attract people from all over the world to its brand of the 'American dream', Japan has yet to define a vision of itself that attracts others to it.

Epilogue: Japan in the 21st century

The frontier within: a spiritual revolution

As was the case in many nations around the world, the turn of the new millennium was an opportunity for reflection in Japan. The 20th century had witnessed its remarkable and tumultuous emergence as a leading, modern nation on the world stage. And yet surveys of public opinion and professional reflection revealed a less than buoyant atmosphere. The last hundred years had seen the establishment of a nation-state, the development of modern industry, a huge but ill-fated regional empire, devastation, and then miraculous economic success, but the heaviest shadow over the millennium was cast by the 1990s – the so-called 'lost decade'. Indeed, far from being the post-industrial techno-utopia envisioned during the confident heights of the 1980s, Japanese society seemed wracked by anxieties and insecurities about its identity and place in the world. Various public surveys showed that levels of happiness and satisfaction were low, and suicide rates in Japan were amongst the highest in the world.

Yet, despite the angst and uncertainty of the 1990s, 21st-century Japan remains one of the most affluent and comfortable societies in the world. Its GDP (at approximately $4.5 trillion) is second only to that of the USA, although by purchasing power parity it is now third behind the USA and China. After a decade of stagnation, the Japanese economy started to grow again in 2003.

Hence, at the turn of the millennium concern for the future vied with retrospection about the past. Under Prime Minister Obuchi, the government established a commission on 'Japan's Goals in the 21st Century', with the self-conscious mission of envisioning a way to avoid (or escape from) Japan's apparent decline. The committee drew on people from various walks of life, ranging from an astronaut to a playwright, but conspicuous by their absence were the bureaucrats of the government ministries. Indeed, public confidence in the government and its apparatus had been decimated in the 1990s: the bursting of the economic bubble, the ongoing collapse of the 'sacred treasures' of Japan's employment system (lifetime employment and seniority-based wages), a stuttering and ineffective international role, and revelations of numerous corruption scandals and factional infighting had completely destroyed the political elite's image of infallibility. The first thing on many people's list of demands for reform was the government itself.

In the end, the committee returned a report in January 2000, 'The Frontier Within: Individual Empowerment and Better Governance in the New Millennium'. The recommendations of the report were far-ranging and profound, and they touched off a period of intensive debate about the condition of Japanese society and its aspirations – a debate that remains unresolved to this day.

The committee made a powerful argument that Japanese society and its morality had been ossified by a 'catch-up' mentality, and hence that it had lost its sense of purpose after its standard of living had actually overtaken that of the so-called West. They argued that Japan must now define an autonomous role for itself, not defined in terms of the West (or especially the USA) but by strengthening its cultural and social ties with East Asia, and supporting the development of multilateral institutions in the region. This idea of a 'return to Asia' has become powerful (if contested) in the public discourse, and a number of commentators have connected it back to Japan's ongoing attempts to 'overcome modernity' by moving through and then transcending the trappings of 'Westernization'. Implicit in this position is the notion that Japan should attract others to it because of the wealth of its own historical and cultural traditions, rather than relying on its ability to seem familiar to people in the West. Japan should claim its modernity for its own. If there is an 'American dream', then there should be a distinctive 'Japanese dream'.

However, the 2000 report was not only a call for cultural confidence and increased patriotism, it was also critical of postwar Japan's introspective tendencies. Against the background of so-called *Nihonjinron* literature, which seeks to establish Japan as a unique, exclusive, and homogeneous polity, the committee argued that Japanese society had lost sight of the fact that its ideal should be egalitarian rather than homogenous: people in Japan should be equal, but this should not come at the price of sacrificing originality, innovation, and individual talent. They severely criticized the strict education system for 'excessive homogeneity and uniformity', which they claimed had produced a work force of servitors rather than innovators, and hence undermined economic and cultural strength. This was an argument that met with considerable support from the public as well as educators, but the committee's recommendation that compulsory education at school could be restricted to three days per week (so that the remaining time could be dedicated to creative individualism) was not taken very seriously.

Finally, the committee was also critical of what they saw as Japanese society's exclusivity. In the background were ongoing issues of prejudice and discrimination against various ethnic minorities (especially Korean immigrants, but also immigrants from Southeast Asia and South America), indigenous peoples (such as the Ainu and Okinawans), social minorities (such as the *burakumin*), and also, in various ways, women. Aside from the moral and ethical issues, which remain serious, the committee was also clear this was of instrumental importance for Japan: a combination of rapidly declining birth rates and great longevity (Japan's average life expectancy of nearly 82 years is the highest in the world), together with a net immigration rate of almost zero, has led to a dangerous 'greying' of Japanese society – approximately 15% of the population is over 65. In fact, Japan's population pyramid is inverted: in 2005, birth rates and death rates in Japan actually coincided; in 2007, Japan's population actually shrank for the first time since the war (to approximately 127,435,000). The greying of Japanese society may represent the greatest threat to economic and social prosperity in 21st-century Japan.

Hence, the committee argued that Japan needed to become more open to immigration and to make more 'equal' use of the various minorities that were already present in the country. This would require both legal and, perhaps more importantly, sociocultural reform.

Of course, the quest to make Japan more attractive for immigration is at least partly dependent upon the success of society's attempts to re-imagine Japanese identity. And the report argues that Japan's first priority in the 21st century should be the start of a spiritual revolution, implying that the 'lost' 1990s represented a rite of passage into a 'second postwar period'. However, the committee also recognized that there were a number of very practical measures that could be taken: it suggested that the Japanese language itself was a potential barrier to Japan's internationalization, and hence that Japan could improve its international profile and make itself more accessible to the world by adopting English as an official second language.

The land of the rising sun

In various attempts to pull itself out of the slump, the first decade of the third millennium has seen Japan undergo a series of social, political, and economic reforms, albeit not always in the manner recommended by the 2000 committee.

The political system itself was restructured in 2001, reducing the power and number of the ministries and focusing more authority in the hands of the prime minister himself. The first beneficiary of this new system was the charismatic Koizumi Jun'ichirô, who was prime minister from 2001 to 2006. Koizumi sought to use the newly empowered office of prime minister to rise above the factional infighting that characterized the politics of the ruling Liberal Democratic Party, and he pushed for a series of radical reforms in both domestic and foreign policy: he oversaw the gradual recovery of the Japanese economy, the beginning of a new national confidence, and he ordered the Self Defence Forces (SDFs) to support US initiatives in the so-called War on Terror, following the events of 11 September 2001. Japan's Anti-Terrorism Act gave the SDFs unprecedented freedoms of manoeuvre beyond Japan's borders.

Koizumi may be remembered as an unusually hawkish and confident prime minister, who rode the wave of the public's need for a new Japanese identity at a time of chronic insecurity. For instance, he was the first postwar Japanese prime minister to visit Yasukuni shrine (to Japan's war dead) and to sign the visitor's book as 'Koizumi Jun'ichirô, the Prime Minister of Japan'. This provoked immediate and dramatic protests from Japan's neighbours, but Koizumi was unapologetic, insisting that patriotism was a healthy and normal part of any national polity.

In fact, Koizumi made a deliberate and innovative attempt to walk the tightrope between placating regional resentments and cultivating national confidence: as well as visiting Yasukuni, Koizumi called for the Self Defence Agency to be turned into a fully fledged Ministry of Defence, pushed the SDFs to collaborate with the USA in unprecedented ways, and urged schools to become more involved in teaching patriotism; but at the same time, Koizumi sought to consolidate Japan's relationships in Asia by making official apologies for the damage caused by Japan during the Pacific War.

In many ways, Koizumi pushed Japan forcefully in the direction of international 'normalcy', following the discussions of the 1990s. However, such an uncompromising stance won Koizumi many enemies as well as supporters, both within Japan and beyond; he was, by turns, Japan's most popular postwar prime minister and its least popular. The legacy of his reforms has yet to be properly understood, but his successor, Abe Shinzô, pushed forward certain aspects of his agenda. Most notably, he oversaw the creation of the Ministry of Defence and the enactment of the Educational Reform Law in December 2006, which requires schools to devote more time to patriotism in class and by singing the national anthem and flying the national flag. He also called for revision of Article 9 of the constitution.

Unlike Koizumi, however, Abe was never a popular prime minister and he resigned suddenly in the autumn of 2007, underlining the fact that Japanese society remains profoundly conflicted about these issues of national identity, and especially military involvement. In October 2008, for instance, General Tamogami Toshio, Air Self Defence Force chief of staff, faced being sacked by Defence Minister Hamada Yasukazu for writing an article in which he said: 'we need to realise that many Asian countries take a positive view of the Greater East Asia War ... it is certainly a false accusation to say that our country was an aggressor nation'. Minister Hamada made a public statement that General Tamogami was out of touch with the position of the government and so should be removed.

Meanwhile, Japanese society has witnessed a host of other reforms. In the sphere of education, it was not only the school system that was reformed from above, the university system was also transformed in response to the problems of the greying society and the so-called 'creativity deficit'. A series of changes to the status and funding of public universities was designed to increase competition between the best universities and promote creativity in research. In addition, leading private universities, such as Keiô University in Tokyo, announced new mission statements 'for the 21st century', declaring their ambitions to develop a more internationalized sense of their intellectual and entrepreneurial responsibilities.

Nonetheless, the elite universities have retained their privileged positions as training grounds for the nation's future leaders, and access to these universities remains intensely meritocratic in principle; the best universities have been known to hold their entrance exams in sports stadiums to accommodate the numbers of applicants. However, principle and practice often diverge: success in the ever-more-demanding entrance exams is increasingly reliant upon the financial means of parents to put their children into specialist 'cram schools' in the evenings, at weekends, and during the 'school vacations'. Hence, the meritocratic ideals are undermined by the realities of a society that is not as homogeneous as its image suggests: income disparities (in a nation where 90% of people consider themselves to be middle class) have grown significantly since Koizumi's economic reforms – indeed, redressing this issue has become part of the policy platform of the main opposition party, the Democratic Party of Japan. Ethnic and social minorities, as well as children from single-parent families, are seriously under-represented in the university system.

Despite the ongoing elitism of the education system, employment patterns have undergone marked changes. With the era of high growth little more than a fading memory, employers are increasingly reluctant to guarantee 'life employment', which means that the rationale for employee loyalty has been undermined. The result is that younger employees are now more likely to change jobs when they are dissatisfied, rather than to stay in the hope of deferred gratification. Hence, the employment market has become rather more fluid.

In turn, relative de-emphasis on the work place as the primary focus of self-identity has led to a re-inscribing of consumer subcultures, particularly amongst the youth of Japan. The most famous and visible (but certainly not the only) of these subcultures might be the so-called *otaku* (geek), characterized by the (usually male) social introvert who spends most of their time and money in an obsessive pursuit of specific artefacts of popular culture, such as anime, manga, or video games. Cultural theorist Azuma Hiroki has referred to '*otaku* culture' as leading Japan into the postmodern world. However, for others this diverse group is the focus of occasional 'panics' about the hollowing out of urban Japanese society, the most recent of which centred on a multiple stabbing in Akihabara (the electronics district of Tokyo) in June 2008. In some ways, this social tension is emblematic of a general sense of unease and distrust between generations.

In addition to various subcultural movements, 21st-century Japan is home to a range of so-called 'new religions', many of which saw resurgence during the 1990s. The most (in)famous (but unrepresentative) of these was *Aum Shinrikyô*, the perpetrators of the sarin gas attacks on the Tokyo subway in 1995. Most of these groups are syncretic religious movements, combining elements of Shintô, Buddhism, and various folk beliefs. In fact, contemporary Japanese society has a complicated relationship with religion; a 2005 survey reported that 80%

of Japanese observed Shintô rituals and ceremonies *and* that nearly 70% considered themselves to be Buddhist.

This combination of consumerist subcultures and spiritual commitments seems to be a feature of 21st-century Japan's sprawling urban environments. Indeed, contemporary Japan is an almost entirely urban society, with only 5% of the population engaged in agriculture and with much of the rest crammed into the approximately 20% of the archipelago that is habitable, with 35 million living in Tokyo-Yokohama alone, making it the most populous metropolis in the world.

These densely packed urban environments bring with them a host of social, economic, and environmental issues, many of which are common to other industrial societies. There are tremendous pressures on health services, especially in terms of provision for the elderly, and on public works. The energy needs of the cities are huge. The transport infrastructures of Japan's cities are stretched to breaking point; the populist image of station attendants in white gloves physically pushing commuters into already stuffed subway trains is not a myth. Roads are similarly overcrowded, with 58 million cars on them. Hence, commutes into work are long and uncomfortable – about a third of all workers and students have to commute for an hour or more. Property prices in the cities are often prohibitively high, and Tokyo is still the most expensive city in the world (although some measures now give this dubious honour to Moscow). Many commentators attribute the high levels of social dissatisfaction to alienation occasioned by these urban woes.

One of the side-effects of this highly developed urbanization has been the rediscovery and re-enchantment of the Japanese countryside, which has become the focus of popular fantasies about the secret and endangered soul of modern Japan. Indeed, the government has even launched campaigns to encourage urbanites to spend more time in rural Japan, not only to improve their quality of life but also to bring them back into contact with a side of Japanese life that they feared was vanishing under the unstoppable wave of urban capitalism. Popular culture, including the world-famous *anime* of Miyazaki Hayao, has been complicit in this representation of a fantastical rural Japan, somehow preserved from the forces of modernity and held in the condition of a pristine and mythical past.

In this respect, it is interesting to reflect on the way the BBC represented Japan during the 2002 World Cup (in the introduction of this book). To some extent, the montage of the old and the new, the geisha and the bullet-train, Mount Fuji and neon streets, is actually a fairly accurate picture of some of the interleaving elements that comprise modern Japan. The key is to remember that this complicated and diverse society is not a fictional 'Eastern' society struggling with features of 'Westernization', but rather a modern society that is continuously negotiating its identity and role in a world of global capitalism. Its modernity is its own. Like many other such societies at the start of the 21st century, a pressing question for Japan is what happens after modernity, and what will be Japan's role in finding out.

Further reading

General on modern Japan

W. G. Beasley, *Rise of Modern Japan: Political, Economic and Social Change since 1850*, 3rd edn. (Weidenfeld & Nicolson, 2000)

Andrew Gordon, *A Modern History of Japan: From Tokugawa Times to the Present* (Oxford University Press, 2003)

Marius Jansen, *The Making of Modern Japan* (Harvard University Press, 2000)

Tokugawa Japan

Harry Harootunian, *Things Seen and Unseen: Discourse and Ideology in Tokugawa Nativism* (University of Chicago Press, 1988)

J. Victor Koschmann, *The Mito Ideology: Discourse, Reform, and Insurrection in Late Tokugawa Japan* (University of California Press, 1987)

Herman Ooms, *Tokugawa Ideology: Early Constructs* (Princeton University Press, 1985)

Conrad Totman, *Politics in the Tokugawa Bakufu* (University of California Press, 1988)

Bob Tadashi Wakabayashi, *Anti-Foreignism and Western Learning in Early-Modern Japan* (Harvard University Press, 1986)

Meiji Japan

Carol Gluck, *Japan's Modern Myths: Ideology in the Late Meiji
Period* (Princeton University Press, 1985)

Marius Jansen, *Sakamoto Ryôma and the Meiji Restoration*
(Stanford University Press, 1961)

Kenneth Pyle, *The New Generation in Meiji Japan* (Stanford
University Press, 1969)

Patricia Tsurumi, *Factory Girls: Women in the Thread Mills of
Meiji Japan* (Princeton University Press, 1990)

George Wilson, *Patriots and Redeemers in Japan: Motives in the
Meiji Restoration* (University of Chicago Press, 1992)

Taishô and early Shôwa Japan

Andrew Barshay, *State and Intellectual in Imperial Japan*
(University of California Press, 1989)

John Dower, *War without Mercy: Race and Power in the Pacific
War* (Pantheon Books, 1986)

Christopher Goto-Jones, *Political Philosophy in Japan: Nishida,
the Kyoto School and Co-Prosperity* (Routledge, 2005)

Harry Harootunian, *Overcome by Modernity: History, Culture,
and Community in Interwar Japan* (Princeton University Press,
2001)

Germaine Hoston, *Marxism and the Crisis of Development in
Prewar Japan* (Princeton University Press, 1986)

Postwar Japan

Gary Allison, *Japan's Postwar History*, 2nd edn. (Cornell University
Press, 2004)

John Dower, *Embracing Defeat: Japan in the Wake of World War II*
(W. W. Norton, 1999)

Andrew Gordon, *The Wages of Affluence: Labor and Management
in Postwar Japan* (Harvard University Press, 1998)

Koichi Iwabuchi, *Recentering Globalization: Popular Culture
and Japanese Transnationalism* (Duke University Press, 2002)

Chalmers Johnson, *MITI and the Japanese Miracle* (Stanford
University Press, 1982)

Rikki Kertsen, *Democracy in Postwar Japan: Maruyama Masao and the Search for Autonomy* (Routledge, 1996)

Masao Miyoshi (ed.), *Postmodernism and Japan* (Duke University Press, 1989)

J. A. A. Stockwin, *Governing Japan: Divided Politics in a Resurgent Economy* (Blackwell Publishing, 2008)

John Treat, *Writing Ground Zero: Japanese Literature and the Atomic Bomb* (University of Chicago Press, 1995)

Index

L

M

N

Modern Japan

Visit the
VERY SHORT INTRODUCTIONS
Web Sites

www.oup.com/uk/vsi
www.oup.com/us

➤ **Information** about all published titles

➤ News of **forthcoming books**

➤ **Extracts** from the books, including titles not yet published

➤ **Reviews** and views

➤ **Links** to other **web sites** and main OUP web page

➤ Information about **VSIs in translation**

➤ **Contact** the editors

➤ **Order** other **VSIs** on-line

Expand your collection of
VERY SHORT INTRODUCTIONS

POLITICS
A Very Short Introduction
Kenneth Minogue

In this provocative but balanced essay, Kenneth Minogue discusses the development of politics from the ancient world to the twentieth century. He prompts us to consider why political systems evolve, how politics offers both power and order in our society, whether democracy is always a good thing, and what future politics may have in the twenty-first century.

'This is a fascinating book which sketches, in a very short space, one view of the nature of politics … the reader is challenged, provoked and stimulated by Minogue's trenchant views.'

Ian Davies, *Talking Politics*

'a dazzling but unpretentious display of great scholarship and humane reflection'

Neil O'Sullivan, University of Hull

www.oup.co.uk/vsi/politics